python
powered

Learning Python

A course in 16 lessons for GCSE

This book aims to be a course study text for those students who study GCSE or IGCSE Computer Science. It is intended to supplement a more general Computer Science text. It can be used in schools as a text to learn programming. Alternatively, it can be used at home for self-study.

Tony Hawken

Learning Python: A course in 16 lessons for GCSE

by Tony Hawken

First published 2017

Copyright: © Tony Hawken 2017

Tony Hawken has asserted his right under the Copyright Designs and Patents act 1988 To be identified as the author of this work.

All rights reserved. No part of this work may be reproduced in any form or by any means, electronic or mechanical, including photocopying, or by any information storage or retrieval system without prior written permission of the copyright owner.

ISBN: 978-1-326-99731-1

Contents

Preface v

Lesson 1: Getting started

1.1	Setting up your programming environment	1
1.2	Using the IDLE shell	3
1.3	Writing a program in script mode	5
1.4	Getting help	9
	Exercise 1	10

Lesson 2: Some arithmetic and variables

2.1	Arithmetic operators	11
2.2	Order of operations	13
2.3	Variables and assignment	15
2.4	A first look at problem-solving	17
2.5	Variable names and keywords	19
	Exercise 2	20

Lesson 3: Strings

3.1	Introducing strings	21
3.2	Special characters, and other features of strings	24
3.3	String functions and methods	25
3.4	Characters and their representation	26
3.5	A programming problem involving strings	27
	Exercise 3	28

Lesson 4: More about data types in Python

4.1	Introduction to data types continued	29
4.2	The data type Boolean and relational operators	30
4.3	Logical connectives and truth tables	33
4.4	Type casting	34
	Exercise 4	36

Lesson 5: Keyboard input, output, and sequence

5.1	Introduction to sequential programming	37
5.2	Keyboard input	39
5.3	Another programming problem with keyboard input	41
5.4	Problem solving	43
	Exercise 5	46

Lesson 6:		Selection – making a choice	
	6.1	Selection using the if statement	47
	6.2	Quadratic equations revisited	49
	6.3	Validation and verification	50
	6.4	Problem solving: Days in a month	52
		Exercise 6	55

Lesson 7:		A first look at lists	
	7.1	Introduction	57
	7.2	Creating and using lists of numbers	58
	7.3	Other ways to create lists	61
		Exercise 7	62

Lesson 8:		Iteration	
	8.1	repeating a fixed number of times	63
	8.2	Use of the `range()` function in for loops	65
	8.3	While loops as an alternative to for loops	67
	8.4	Using a while loop to terminate input	68
	8.5	Terminating a while loop when a value has been reached	69
	8.6	Using a break to terminate a loop	70
	8.7	Nested loops	71
		Exercise 8	72

Lesson 9:		Functions	
	9.1	A first look at functions in Python	73
	9.2	More examples of functions that return a value	74
	9.3	Functions with no return statement	76
	9.4	Local variables and scope	79
	9.5	Palindromes	80
	9.6	Recursive functions	82
		Exercise 9	84

Lesson 10:		Using lists as arrays	
	10.1	Introduction	85
	10.2	Examples of array processing	87
	10.3	Using functions to process arrays	88
	10.4	Functions that return an array	90
	10.5	Two-dimensional lists (arrays)	92
		Exercise 10	94

Lesson 11: Using Files

11.1	Introduction	95
11.2	reading from a file	96
11.3	Writing to a file	99
11.4	Using functions to process files	102
	Exercise 11	104

Lesson 12: A mathematical interlude

12.1	Standard form	105
12.2	The math module	106
12.3	Trigonometry	107
12.4	Random numbers	109
12.5	Numerical solution of a cubic equation	112
12.6	Very large prime numbers	114
	Exercise 12	116

Lesson 13: Algorithms, flowcharts, and pseudo-code

13.1	Flow charts	117
13.2	Flow charts and pseudo-code for programming constructs	119
13.3	Programming design with structure charts	122
13.4	Jackson structured programming	125
	Exercise 13	128

Lesson 14: Searching and sorting

14.1	Linear search	129
14.2	Binary search	130
14.3	Bubble sort	131
14.4	Merging two lists	133
14.5	Merge sort	135
14.6	Insertion sort	136
14.7	Sorting algorithms profiling	138
	Exercise 14	140

Lesson 15: Dealing with errors

15.1	Introduction	141
15.2	Syntax errors	142
15.3	Run-time errors	144
15.4	Logic errors	145
15.5	Using a trace table and other debugging methods	146
15.6	Designing a test plan	150
	Exercise 15	152

Lesson 16: Non examination assessment

16.1	Check for valid ISBNs	153
16.2	Binary numbers converted to base 10	156
16.3	Hexadecimal numbers converted to base 10	159
16.4	A simple film database	161
	Exercise 16	168

Appendix A: Bibliography   169

Appendix B: Resources   170

Index   171

Preface

Acknowledgements

Firstly, I would like to thank John Davis for his perseverance and encouragement. He has painstakingly proof-read all chapters in this book and provided me with comprehensive notes on how I can improve the book. He has picked up many typos and in the main has corrected my grammar and made other suggestions to improve the readability of the text.

I also have to acknowledge that I have benefited by reading a number of Python books. It is from these books that I have learnt Python. Many of these are listed in the bibliography. The most credit must go to "Python for software design: How to program like a computer scientist" by Allen B. Downey. It is this book that I read when I went to look after my mum for a week. It was a means to block out the day-time television, and it did give me a very good basic understanding of Python.

Finally, I have to remember those teachers who have made a lasting impression on me. I have to thank Jim Inglis and Keith Mannock for their inspirational teaching whilst I was studying at Birkbeck College. Although this was a long time ago, and much of the Computer Science I learnt is now well out-of-date, there are key ideas that they taught me that are still relevant today.

Who is this book for?

The primary intended audience for this book are those students that are studying or intend to study GCSE Computer Science. The content of the book closely follows the programming requirements of the main exam boards – AQA, EDEXCEL, and OCR. There are topics that are not covered in the book that are requirements for the WJEC Computer Science. So, Classes and object-oriented programming is not covered. I have also checked out the syllabi for IGCSE. This book covers the programming content for these as well.

Whilst doing research online, it has become apparent to me that as well as students who are studying GCSE Computer Science, it is also often taught to students studying at key stage 3. It is possible that these students may derive some benefit from the book.

Finally, it can be used by anyone who wishes to learn to program in Python.

Aims of the book:

The main aim for this book is to encourage people to program. It is written in a style that encourages students to experiment and try things out. The earlier chapters almost exclusively use the Python shell. In these cases, students will only ever type in a line or two of code at a time. It is giving them the opportunity to try things out to see what will happen.

In later chapters, programs are typed in using an editor in script mode. Many of these programs are very short, rarely more than 10 lines long. The longer programs appear towards the end of the book. To carry out a non exam assessment, students are expected to write longer programs. There are some examples of what I consider to be a suitable assessment in the last chapter of the book. The largest of these programs has 72 lines of code. I have always gone along with the KISS principle – "Keep it simple, stupid". That is, programs should be short and simple. They should also be easy to understand.

The title of this book would suggest that it is a book to be used in the class room. That is my intention. I would suggest that students do no more than one chapter (lesson) per week. Studied this way, a student can learn Python in 4 months. It is a fact, these days students do not like to read. Also, schools do not use text-books for the bulk of their lessons. That is a pity. A good text book provides a structure and content that make life easier for both student and teacher.

I would like to think that this could become a core book to learn the programming skills necessary for studying GCSE Computer Science.

Why use Python?

There are very many reasons for using Python as a first programming language. These include:

- Python is much easier to learn than most other languages
- Python programs tend to be very short
- Python syntax encourages you to write good code
- Python is an incredibly powerful and efficient language
- Python is used in a wide range of applications
- Python is taught in many schools at KS3 and for GCSE and A level Computer Science
- Python is taught in many university departments
- Python is used in industry
- There is a new subject that can be studied at university called Data Science. Here you would be expected to program in Python.

All of the GCSE exam boards support the use of Python for programming. Many of the languages offered though are far too difficult. How about having to learn Java? I did once teach Java on an INSET course to IT teachers in a FE college. Many of these teachers dropped out before lunch time.

If you look at the positive qualities of other approved languages and compare them with the reasons for using Python listed above, most of the other languages would fail abysmally. It is a no-brainer – Python should be the language to choose.

Lesson 1: Getting started

1.1 Setting up you programming environment

I will be using this chapter to acquaint you with the Python programming environment. I will also be suggesting how you should set up your facilities for ease of use. I will be using the standard Python distribution that can be found at:

https://www.python.org/downloads/

In this book I will be using Python 3.4 as it is compatible with my older Windows operating system. Feel free to obtain the latest download that will suit your computer and operating system. There will not be any noticeable differences with the sub-set of Python I will be using. Make sure that you download Python 3, not Python 2, because these are somewhat different.

I will not be telling you how to install the Python software, even though many books do. It is a question of clicking on the download link, then clicking on the file that you have just downloaded. It more or less installs itself. Installation of this software is very intuitive.

Once installed, I want you to set up a workspace for you to do your programming. This involves a basic knowledge of using Windows.

We will start by creating a folder to store your programs. You start by right-clicking the mouse. You will obtain a menu as follows. Now click on **New**, and choose **folder**.

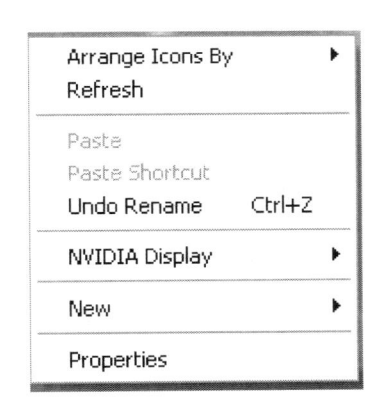

You will now get something like this.

It is up to you to enter an appropriate name. I am going to call it "My Python programs".

This is your programming workspace. You can place in here your programs and other objects that will help with your programming.

If you do this, you should end up with the following.

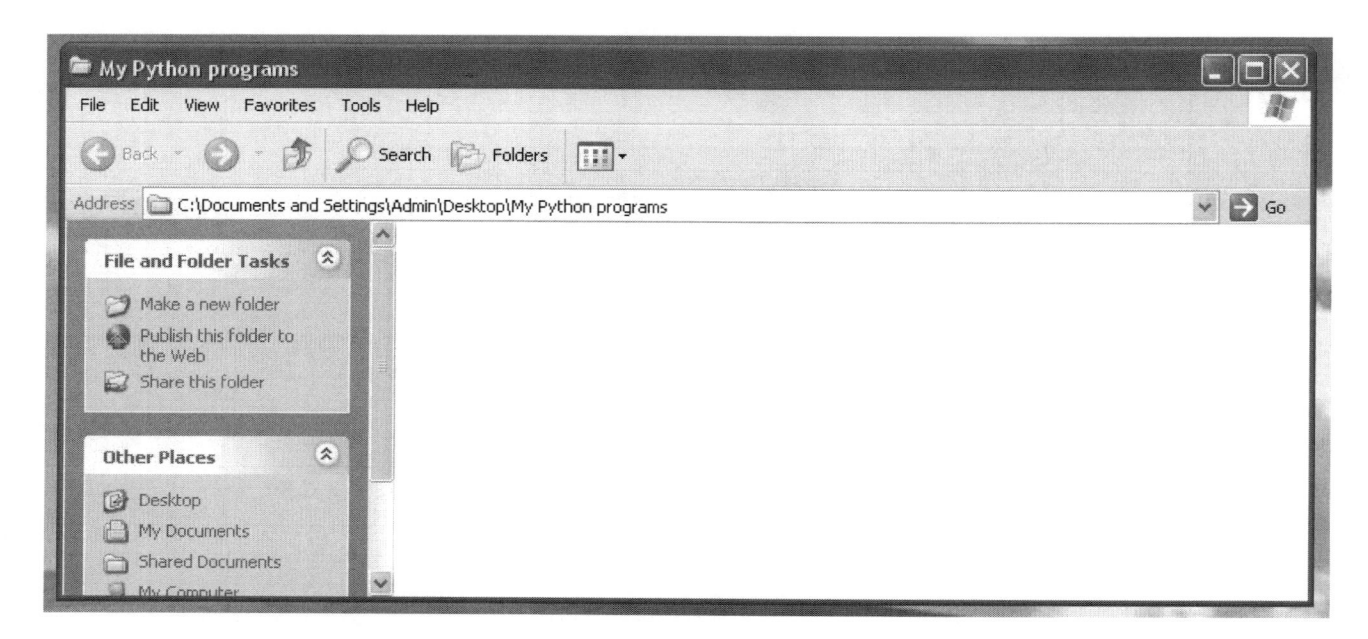

I will at this stage suggest that it would be very useful if you had a shortcut to load the Python software. The easiest way to do this is to drag an existing shortcut for Python into your folder.

If you click on the Start button, you may see something like this.

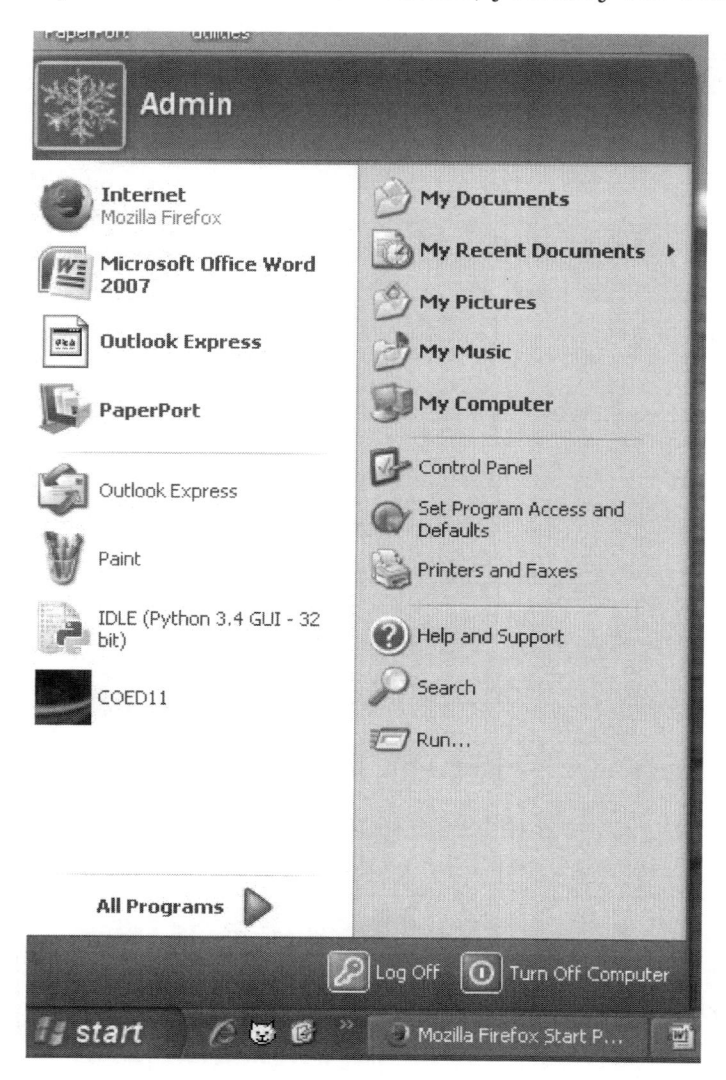

You can see that there is an icon for IDLE (Python 3.4 GUI – 32 bit). If not you will have to search for it by clicking on **All Programs**.

IDLE is the name of the **Interactive Development Environment** (IDE) that we will be using. You probably know what GUI stands for. But, I will tell you anyway. It stands for **Graphic User Interface**. A GUI typically is a user interface that allows you to use a mouse as well as a keyboard. It also has many features that you associate with the Windows operating system.

You can now left-click this icon and drag it to your folder before releasing the mouse button.

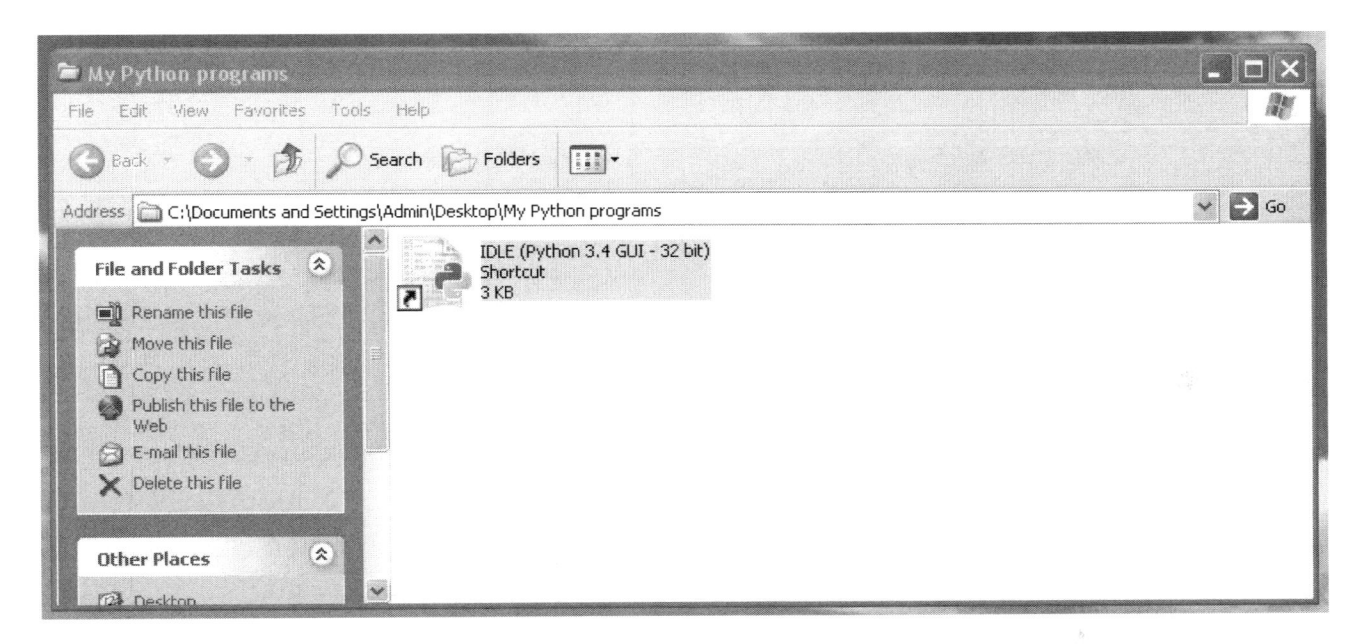

Now, when you want to use the Python IDE, just click on this icon.

If you are using Python at school, things may be rather different. If you are stuck make sure you ask your teacher for help.

1.2 Using the IDLE shell

We are now going to have a preliminary look at the Python IDLE environment. We start by clicking on the icon we have in our folder. You should obtain something like this.

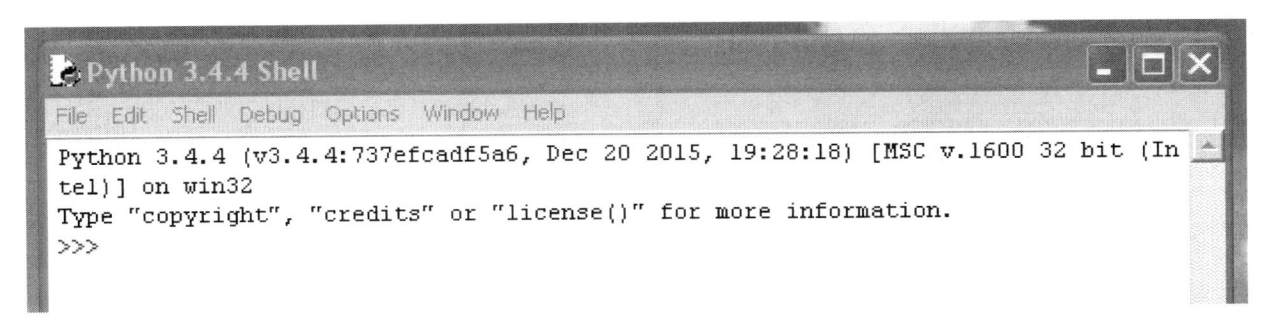

This is the Python shell. It is used for interactive programming. You will notice at the bottom of the picture >>>. This is the **command prompt**. Each time you see one of these, you can type in a command or statement. This command or statement will be

3

executed if possible. It may not be possible if you have made a mistake. In this case you will get an error message instead.

The IDLE shell is a very basic **interpreter**. For each command typed in, the command is translated (interpreted) and executed.

We will start by entering some simple expressions to see what happens.

```
Python 3.4.4 Shell
File  Edit  Shell  Debug  Options  Window  Help
Python 3.4.4 (v3.4.4:737efcadf5a6, Dec 20 2015, 19:28:18) [MSC v.1600 32 bit (In
tel)] on win32
Type "copyright", "credits" or "license()" for more information.
>>> 'Hello, world!'
'Hello, world!'
>>> 2
2
>>> 4.6
4.6
>>> 2 + 3
5
>>> 12 / 4
3.0
>>>
```

To start with, I have entered the string, 'Hello, world!'. I have then pressed return. The expression is evaluated. In response you get a copy of the string. A **string** is merely a sequence of characters enclosed between either single, or double quotes.

I have done the same with numbers.

I start with the **integer** 2. An integer is another name for a whole number. You can tell whether a number is an integer - it does not have a decimal point in it. Obviously the number 2 evaluates to 2.

Next is a **real number** – it does have a decimal point. As far as python is concerned, and this is so with most other programming languages, a number with a decimal point in it is a real number. In many programming languages including python, real numbers are called **floating point numbers** or **floats**. This is how they are implemented.

You can see from what follows, that I can also use the IDLE shell as a calculator.

The expression 2 + 3 indicates that the numbers are being added. Python correctly evaluates this sum to be equal to 5.

The next statement shows real division. The operator / is equivalent to the more familiar ÷ sign that we see in basic mathematics. I say that it is real division, because the answer is always a real number. The number 3.0 has a decimal point in it, so it is a real number even if it is equivalent to the number 3.

As you would expect, there are other arithmetic operators. Arithmetic operators will be dealt with in more detail later.

Considering what we have done so far, you may well say this is all very well, but what about writing a program. We do not want to write a program one statement at a time, and have it excecuted before we type in the next statement.

1.3 Writing a program in script mode

If you want to write a program, we can do this by using what is called **script mode**. You enter **script mode** by opening a new window. You do this by Clicking on **File** at the top of the IDLE shell. Then click on **New File**. This will generate a new Window.

I have included a picture to highlight what you have to click.

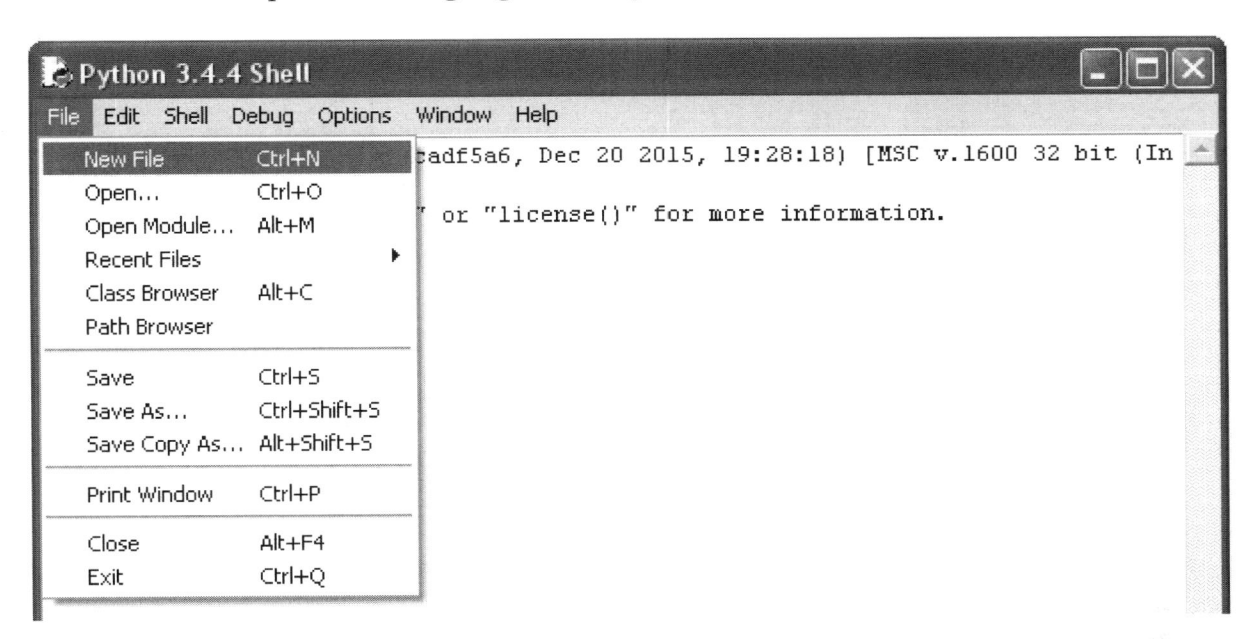

Once you have done this you obtain the following.

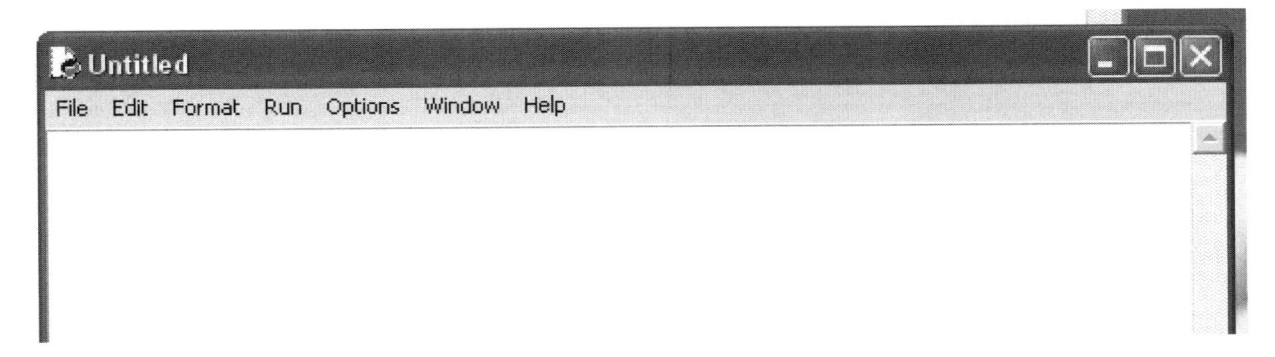

It is here that you can type in, edit and run programs. You have all the facilities that you would expect with an editor such as notepad, but in addition, most importantly, you can run your program.

I am going to write a simple program and step-by-step show you how to save the program and run it.

I will start by typing in a print statement.

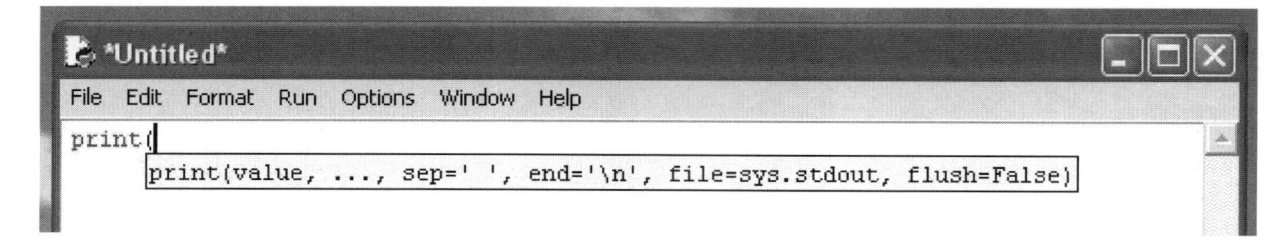

```
*Untitled*
File  Edit  Format  Run  Options  Window  Help
print(
      print(value, ..., sep=' ', end='\n', file=sys.stdout, flush=False)
```

No sooner have I typed `print(`, and I am given a prompt to remind me of the syntax of a print statement. This looks horribly complicated, so we will ignore it for a moment. This feature however is quite common for programming editors. It is like a crib sheet should someone want to know all the features of the print statement.

I did ignore this, and just typed in what I wanted. If you keep on typing the prompt goes away.

```
*Untitled*
File  Edit  Format  Run  Options  Window  Help
print('Hello, World!')
print(2)
print(4 + 6)
print(12 / 4)
```

I have not copied exactly what I typed in when using interactive mode using the Python shell. I have had to put the expressions inside a print statement. This is necessary if I want to output to the screen the values of the expressions.

Before I run this program, I need to save it. To do this, click on **File**, followed by **Save As…**. I have not clicked on **Save As…** at this stage, because I want to make sure that you get this right.

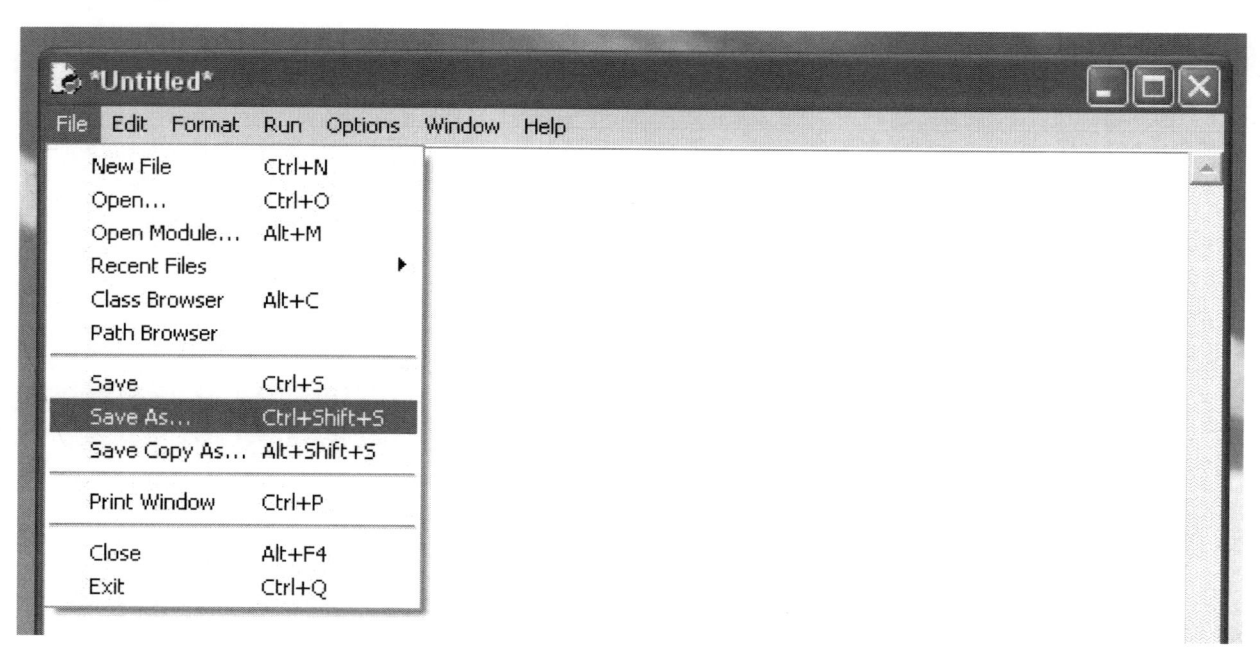

```
*Untitled*
File  Edit  Format  Run  Options  Window  Help
 New File          Ctrl+N
 Open...           Ctrl+O
 Open Module...    Alt+M
 Recent Files            ▶
 Class Browser     Alt+C
 Path Browser
 Save              Ctrl+S
 Save As...        Ctrl+Shift+S
 Save Copy As...   Alt+Shift+S
 Print Window      Ctrl+P
 Close             Alt+F4
 Exit              Ctrl+Q
```

Once you have done this, you get the following. There is a **Save As** window that allows you to specify which folder to save the file in, also the facility to allow you to type in the file name.

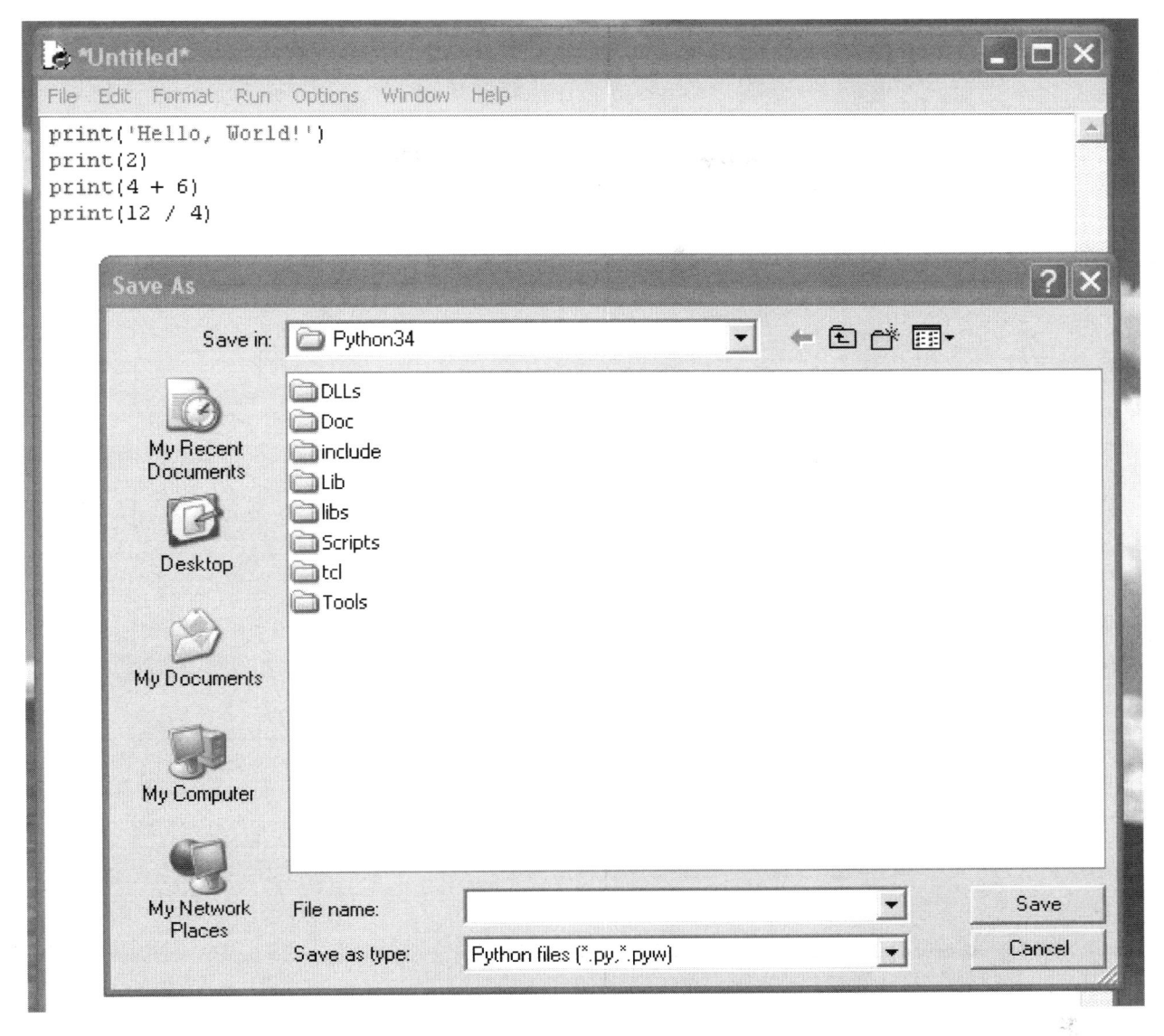

Make sure you locate your folder to save the file in. Search for it using the **Save in:** pop-down menu. Then type in the filename where it says **File Name:**. Then make sure that the file has the .py extension. This indicates that the file contains a Python program.

When you have done this you can click on **Save**. The heading of your IDE will now contain the program name. You now know that it has been saved.

There follows an edited screen dump to show this. Note, I have taken the trouble to display the folder as well. You will notice that there is an icon corresponding to the file that has just been saved.

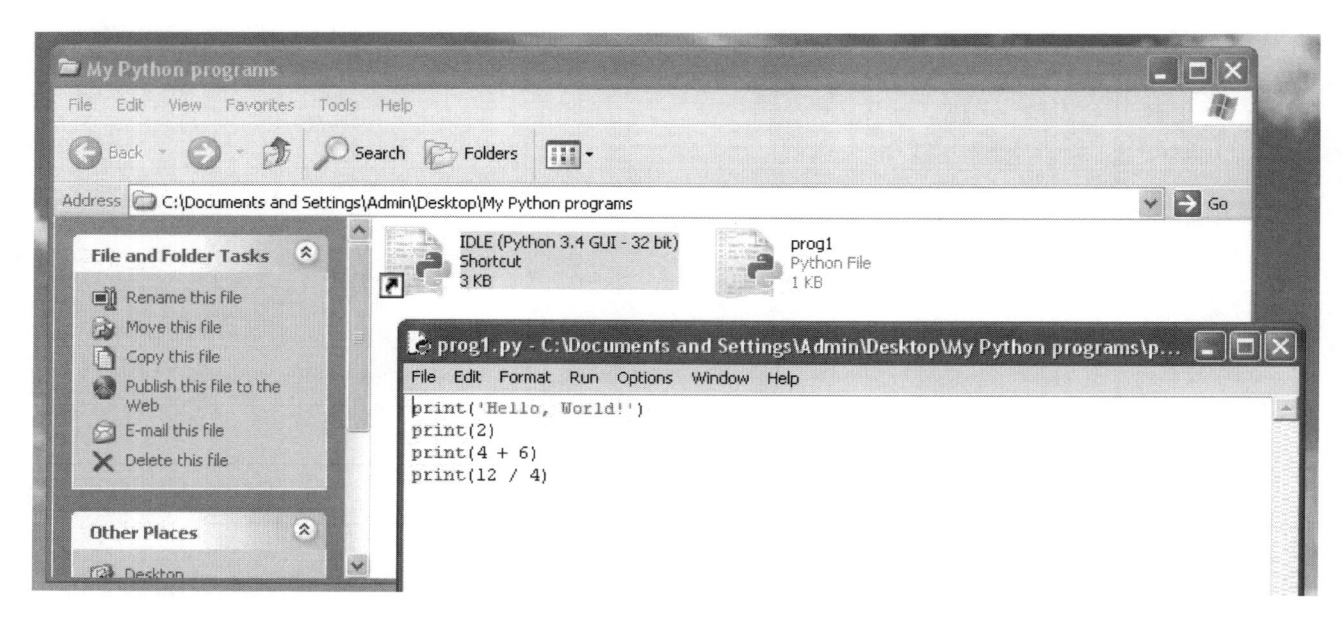

[Screenshot: "My Python programs" folder window showing IDLE shortcut and prog1 Python file, with prog1.py editor open containing:]

```
print('Hello, World!')
print(2)
print(4 + 6)
print(12 / 4)
```

I now intend to run the program. Simply click on **Run**, followed by **Run Module F5**.

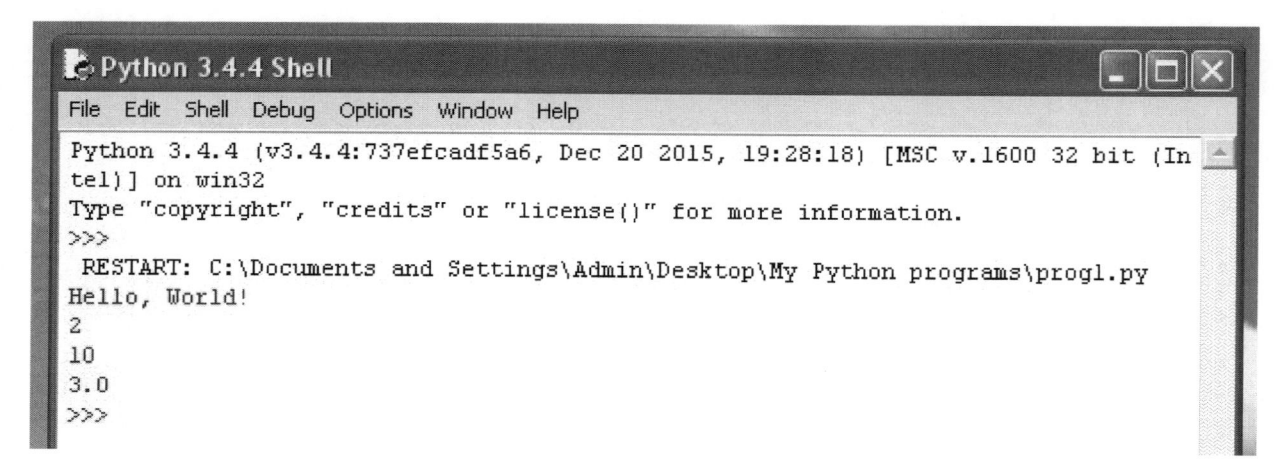

[Screenshot: Python 3.4.4 Shell output:]

```
Python 3.4.4 (v3.4.4:737efcadf5a6, Dec 20 2015, 19:28:18) [MSC v.1600 32 bit (Intel)] on win32
Type "copyright", "credits" or "license()" for more information.
>>> 
 RESTART: C:\Documents and Settings\Admin\Desktop\My Python programs\prog1.py
Hello, World!
2
10
3.0
>>> 
```

Running a program in this manner loads the Python shell. Here the program is interpreted line-by-line and executed. You will notice that the resulting output specifies that program prog1.py is being run. The output from the program is much the same that we obtained by using the Python shell directly. The main difference, is that we had to use print statements to obtain this.

You will be using these skills throughout the book. But, once you have done this, it will seem very straightforward and I will not have to remind you again.

If you want to return to a Python script so that you can edit it, the easiest way involves first locating the icon corresponding to the program file; then right-click your mouse over the icon.

[Screenshot: Right-click context menu on prog1 icon showing:
- Open
- Edit with IDLE (highlighted)
- Add to .7Z
- Add to .ZIP
- Add to archive
- Open as archive]

8

This takes you into the IDLE editor; here you can modify the code before running the program again.

1.4 Getting help

There will come a time when you feel that you do not know what you are doing. It is now time to obtain help. The easiest way to do this is to type `help()` at the command prompt in the interactive shell.

```
>>> help()

Welcome to Python 3.4's help utility!

If this is your first time using Python, you should definitely check out
the tutorial on the Internet at http://docs.python.org/3.4/tutorial/.

Enter the name of any module, keyword, or topic to get help on writing
Python programs and using Python modules.  To quit this help utility and
return to the interpreter, just type "quit".

To get a list of available modules, keywords, symbols, or topics, type
"modules", "keywords", "symbols", or "topics".  Each module also comes
with a one-line summary of what it does; to list the modules whose name
or summary contain a given string such as "spam", type "modules spam".

help>
```

If you follow the instructions given above, you can find out a lot about Python. I will start by typing topics at the help prompt.

```
help> topics

Here is a list of available topics.  Enter any topic name to get more help.

ASSERTION           DELETION            LOOPING             SHIFTING
ASSIGNMENT          DICTIONARIES        MAPPINGMETHODS      SLICINGS
ATTRIBUTEMETHODS    DICTIONARYLITERALS  MAPPINGS            SPECIALATTRIBUTES
ATTRIBUTES          DYNAMICFEATURES     METHODS             SPECIALIDENTIFIERS
AUGMENTEDASSIGNMENT ELLIPSIS            MODULES             SPECIALMETHODS
BASICMETHODS        EXCEPTIONS          NAMESPACES          STRINGMETHODS
BINARY              EXECUTION           NONE                STRINGS
BITWISE             EXPRESSIONS         NUMBERMETHODS       SUBSCRIPTS
BOOLEAN             FLOAT               NUMBERS             TRACEBACKS
CALLABLEMETHODS     FORMATTING          OBJECTS             TRUTHVALUE
CALLS               FRAMEOBJECTS        OPERATORS           TUPLELITERALS
CLASSES             FRAMES              PACKAGES            TUPLES
CODEOBJECTS         FUNCTIONS           POWER               TYPEOBJECTS
COMPARISON          IDENTIFIERS         PRECEDENCE          TYPES
COMPLEX             IMPORTING           PRIVATENAMES        UNARY
CONDITIONAL         INTEGER             RETURNING           UNICODE
CONTEXTMANAGERS     LISTLITERALS        SCOPING
CONVERSIONS         LISTS               SEQUENCEMETHODS
DEBUGGING           LITERALS            SEQUENCES

help>
```

Obviously, if you can see what you are interested in, you can type the item you want.

The other major source of information, is the Internet. A good place to start is the official Python site, and look for tutorials.

If you type Python tutorials within a search engine such as google, you will obtain a large list of links to Python tutorials.

One of them will be called: The Python Tutorial; this is on the official Python site. For convenience I have included the link.

>   https://docs.python.org/3/tutorial/

Exercise 1

1. Create a folder as detailed previously. In it create a shortcut for Python.
2. Click on the Python shortcut, and experiment by typing in expressions in interactive mode using the Python shell. You may encounter some error messages. I will talk about these later. Do not worry about error messages.
3. Type in, and run a short program in script mode using the Python IDE. Don't forget to save it first.

Lesson 2: Some arithmetic and variables

2.1 Arithmetic operators

We will start by looking at some of the arithmetic operators that we are familiar with in the mathematics classroom.

Arithmetic operator	Python operator	Description	Example
+	+	addition	2 + 3
−	−	subtraction	7 − 4
×	*	multiplication	3 * 5
÷	/	Real division	8 / 4
a^n	**	exponentiation	2 ** 5

To demonstrate these operators, I will enter the examples here into the Python shell.

```
>>> 2+3
5
>>> 7-4
3
>>> 3*5
15
>>> 8/4
2.0
>>> 2**5
32
>>>
```

In this case the expressions with add, subtract and multiply do what is expected. In the case of division, 8/4 gives the real number 2.0 and not 2 as you may have expected. All the other operators tried out give an integer answer.

Obviously in the case of the expression 8 / 5, you would expect to obtain an answer that involves a decimal point and hence a real number.

```
>>> 8/5
1.6
>>>
```

With the expression 2**5, you are working out 2 to the power of 5 (2^5). This is equivalent to 2×2×2×2×2.

I will now look at some other operators that you can use with integers.

Arithmetic operator	Python operator	Description	Example
÷	//	integer division	16 // 5
x mod y	%	remainder	16 % 5

To think about integer division, you have to cast your mind back to long division. Here the whole number part of the answer, is the same as the resulting value when you use the operator //. Likewise, the remainder that you obtain by doing long division is the same as the resulting value of an expression that uses the % operator.

```
>>> 16 // 5
3
>>> 16 % 5
1
>>>
```

You can easily verify this yourself by dividing 16 by 5.

You can use the same operators with real numbers. I will just type in a few examples and then explain what is happening.

```
>>> 2+2.5
4.5
>>> 2 + 2.0
4.0
>>> 5 - 3.0
2.0
>>> 2.0 * 3
6.0
>>> 13.5 / 3
4.5
>>> 13.5 // 3
4.0
>>> 13.5 % 3
1.5
>>> 2 ** 1.5
2.8284271247461903
>>>
```

Firstly, any arithmetic expression that contains at least 1 real number will always result in an answer that is a real number, even if that real number is equivalent in value to an integer. For example the real number 4.0 is equivalent to the integer 4.

Even operators such as // and % behave in the way you would expect them to. The only difference is that the result will always be a real number.

This takes some getting use to. If I carried out the following:

4.0 // 2

This will give me the answer 2.0 because one or more of the numbers is a real number.

2.2 Order of operations

Typically in the classroom you have to be able to work out more difficult expressions than this, that contain a number of operators, possibly different operators. If this is the case, the order that you work out the expression is important. There are rules of precedence that determine how expressions should be worked out. In the mathematics classroom the acronyms, BODMAS, PEMDAS and various other permutations are used to help you remember what this order is.

I will just state what the order of precedence is, using a table.

Order (precedence)	Operator
1	brackets ( )
2	exponentiation or powers (2^3 etc)
3	multiply, divide ($\times$, $\div$)
4	add, subtract ($+$, $-$)

To illustrate this, a number of examples follow.

Example 1

$2 + 3 \times 5$

Here we have two operators. The multiplication needs to be done first.

$2 + 3 \times 5 = 2 + 15 = 17$

To work this out using Python, we would type: $2 + 3 * 5$

Example 2

$3(2 \times 4 - 7) + 2 \times 3$

Here the contents of the brackets need to be worked out first. Then inside the brackets, the multiplication needs to be done first.

$3 (2 \times 4 - 7) + 2 \times 3 = 3(8 - 7) + 6 = 3 \times 1 + 6 = 9$

To work this out using Python, we would type: $3 * (2 * 4 - 7) + 2 * 3$

Note that I have included a * between 3 and the first bracket. That is because when you use brackets like this, there is always an implied multiply. We are using the brackets as a means to group things together. A 3 outside the brackets indicates that the contents are multiplied by 3.

Example 3

$3 \times 2^4 + 7$

Here the power needs to be worked out first, followed by multiply, followed by add.

$3 \times 2^4 + 7 = 3 \times 16 + 7 = 48 + 7 = 55$

To work this out in Python, we would type: `3 * 2 ** 4 + 7`

Example 4

$$\frac{7 + \sqrt{16}}{2^3 + 4^3 - 1}$$

This is somewhat trickier to work out. We need to introduce brackets to group items together. We need to indicate that all of the terms on the top, are divided by all of the terms on the bottom. If we include brackets the expression becomes.

$$\frac{(7 + \sqrt{16})}{(2^3 + 4^3 - 1)}$$

$$\frac{(7 + \sqrt{16})}{(2^3 + 4^3 - 1)} = \frac{(7+4)}{(8+64-1)} = \frac{11}{71}$$

To work this out in Python we could type

`(7 + math.sqrt(16) ) / (2 ** 3 + 4 ** 3 - 1)`

Or alternatively

`(7 + 16 ** 0.5 ) / (2 ** 3 + 4 ** 3 - 1)`

In the first instance I have used a standard Python function called `sqrt()` and this is part of the class math. I will have more to say about this later.

In the second instance I have used the fact that $\sqrt{x} = x^{0.5}$

I now want to consider other aspects of order of working out expressions.

How for instance, would I work out the expression 16 - 8 – 4?

In this case we work out 16 – 8 first, then subtract 4. For the operations, add, subtract, multiply and divide Python will always evaluate the expression from left-to-right. In the case of addition, and multiplication, we will get the same answer no matter what order we evaluate the expression. But, in the case of subtraction and division, order is important. For the following we have to work it out like this: 16 – 8 – 4 = 8 – 4 = 4. If we did the subtraction in a different order we would get a different answer. We say that these expressions are left-to-right associative.

However I should note that when you are dealing with powers, this is right-to-left associative.

Consider the expression 2^{2^4}

This is equivalent to $2^{(2^4)}$. Here the brackets are used to indicate that 2^4 is worked out first.

Assuming this is right-to-left associate, the expression:

$$2^{2^4} = 2^{(2^4)} = 2^{16} = 65536$$

If we worked this out incorrectly, that is we assumed it was left-to-right associate we would be working out:

$$(2^2)^4 = 4^4 = 256$$

We can show that the first calculation is correct by using the Python shell.

```
>>> 2 ** 2 ** 4
65536
>>>
```

2.3 Variables and assignment

When we want to write proper programs, we need to have named storage to store intermediate results. For this, we need to introduce **variables**.

In mathematics, a **variable** is a letter that can take a number of values. In the context of programming, a variable is usually thought of as a named piece of storage.

In most other programming languages we need to **declare** a variable before it can be used. For example in C++ we could write the following:

```
int a;
a = 3;
```

The first statement instructs the computer to put aside sufficient storage to store an integer or int. In C++ these days 4 **bytes** is typically used for this purpose. A byte is an 8 bit word.

The second statement stores the number 3 in the piece of storage called a. This is called an **assignment statement**. Here the operator = is referred to as the **assignment operator**. It is telling the computer to store the value 3 into the piece of storage referred to as a.

When programming in Python, you do not declare the variable before you use it. You merely use an assignment statement such as: a = 3 to both create named storage, and place a value in it.

The Python interpreter is able to tell that the value 3 is an integer. The same applies to other data types. Python can work out the type of a variable by comparing it to the type of the value being assigned to the variable.

In the case of the statement b = 3.5, the interpreter knows that b refers to a real, or floating point number, because the number 3.5 has a decimal point in it, and a number with a decimal point is a real number or float.

You can also use the same variable at different stages of the program to refer to data values that have a different type.

So, it is permissible to do the following.

```
>>> a = 3
>>> a
3
>>> a = 3.5
>>> a
3.5
>>> a = "Hello"
>>> a
'Hello'
>>>
```

I would however suggest that you don't do this, as it can make things confusing.

In mathematics, variables are normally present in formulae. An example of such a formula is the formula to convert a temperature in Centigrade to Fahrenheit. It is normally written as

$$F = \frac{9}{5} C + 32$$

To convert a temperature of 25° Centigrade to Fahrenheit, we could write a simple Python program as follows.

```
c = 25
f = 9 / 5 * c + 32
print(f)
```

First c is assigned a value of 25. This value is substituted into the right-hand-side of the expression involving f. The resulting value is stored in f. Finally, the value stored in f is displayed on the screen.

Assignment statements can be used to modify a value that has already been stored. Consider the following statements.

```
n = 5
n = n + 1
```

The first statement creates the variable n, and stores 5 in it. The second statement takes the current value of n, and adds 1 to it. The new value of n will now be 6. In this situation, we say that the variable n has been **incremented** by 1.

Likewise, I can **decrement** a variable by 1 by using the statement that follows.

```
n = n - 1
```

2.4 A first look at problem solving

Suppose 1 want to convert 1 million seconds to days, hours, minute seconds. We will have to start by noting the following:

1 day = 24 hours

1 hour = 60 minutes

1 minute = 60 seconds

So, to get a rough idea of how many days this is we could run the following.

```
>>> seconds = 1000000
>>> minutes = seconds / 60
>>> hours = minutes / 60
>>> days = hours / 24
>>> days
11.574074074074074
>>>
```

This gives us the number of days, but we want to express the answer in the form days, hours, minutes, and seconds.

How can we directly get the number of days, from the number of seconds?

From the statements, above we can see that the number of days is given by:

$$days = \frac{seconds}{60 \times 60 \times 24}$$

We can test this in Python with the following.

```
>>> seconds = 1000000
>>> days = seconds / (60 * 60 * 24)
>>> days
11.574074074074074
>>>
```

Notice, we obtain the same answer. This time we need to make some changes to obtain a whole number of hours. Think of an operator that will only provide me with a whole number of hours and ignore the remainder.

The integer division operator // will do the job. The next problem is that we need to keep the remainder. We could use the operator % to achieve this.

```
>>> seconds = 1000000
>>> days = seconds // (60 * 60 * 24)
>>> days
11
>>> remainder = seconds % (60 * 60 * 24)
>>> remainder
49600
>>>
```

If we were to continue with this idea, we now need to turn the remainder of 49600 seconds into hours and seconds. We can do this as before.

We are now ready to write a complete program. Now that we have tested some of the code, we can be confident to type in a program in script mode. The completed program follows.

```
# A program to convert 1 million seconds to
# days, hours, minutes, and seconds

seconds = 1000000
days = seconds // (60 * 60 * 24)
remainder = seconds % (60 * 60 * 24)
hours = remainder // (60 * 60)
remainder = remainder % (60 * 60)    # New remainder in seconds
minutes = remainder // 60
seconds = remainder % 60             # New remainder in seconds

print("One million seconds is ")
print(days, 'days', hours, 'hours', minutes, 'minutes', seconds, 'seconds')
```

When I run this, I obtain the desired result.

```
>>>
 RESTART: C:/Documents and Settings/Admin/Desktop/My Python programs/problem.py
One million seconds is
11 days 13 hours 46 minutes 40 seconds
>>>
```

You will notice that I have added some things to my program that I have not previously mentioned.

The program now has **comments**. In this case everything that appears after the # symbol is ignored by the Python interpreter. These comments are for people to read, not the interpreter. They are a useful part of the program documentation, and are used to make programs easier to understand.

The print statements are more complicated than I have previously used. The first one just prints a string. The second print statement contains a list of strings and variable names. The contents of strings are printed literally, and the values of the variable names are printed.

You will also note that I have used more meaningful variable names. Instead of just using single letters, I have used variable names that are meaningful. This is also an aid to making programs easier to understand.

2.5 Variable names and keywords

I have not yet said much about variable names. There is a set of rules, which determine what is allowed in Python programs, and what is a sensible choice for a variable name.

I include some necessary rules, and some sensible advice.

All variables must start with a letter. After the first character you can use letters, and numbers. You can also use both uppercase and lowercase letters. I prefer, where possible, only to use lowercase.

You cannot include spaces in a variable name

Variable names can contain an underscore (_). This is often used to separate words where you have two or more words in a variable name. The variable name num_words is an example.

Another way of dealing with the problem of having two or more words in a variable name is to use what is called camel case. That is the next word always starts with an uppercase character. The variable name numWords is an example.

Variable names can be as long as you like, but it is sensible to keep them short.

You cannot use a Python keyword as a variable name. I have included a table with the keywords present in Python 3. You can see that I used `help()` to obtain this.

```
>>> help('keywords')

Here is a list of the Python keywords.  Enter any keyword to get more help.

False               def                 if                  raise
None                del                 import              return
True                elif                in                  try
and                 else                is                  while
as                  except              lambda              with
assert              finally             nonlocal            yield
break               for                 not
class               from                or
continue            global              pass
```

Python is **case-sensitive**, so it is most important to have keywords in the right case. Notice most of the key words are lowercase – 3 start with an uppercase character.

If you are using variables, you must be consistent with the spelling and case. If you start using a variable that is lowercase, you must be consistent and keep the same case and spelling throughout the program.

Exercise 2

1. If the following commands were to be run in interactive mode, explain with reasons what the output would be

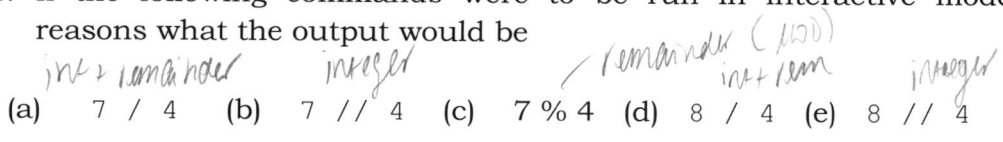

   (a) 7 / 4   (b) 7 // 4   (c) 7 % 4   (d) 8 / 4   (e) 8 // 4

   (f) 4 + 3 * 7   (g) 3 * 2 ** 4 - 1   (h) 600 / 6 / 10

2. Consider the following program. Determine the output.

   ```
   x = 5
   y = 3
   z = 7 + x * y
   a = (7 + x) * y
   b = 10 + (z + x) / y
   c = x * 5 ** 2 + 10
   print(a, b, c)
   ```

3. Write valid Python assignment statements for the following formulae

   (a) $c = \sqrt{a^2 + b^2}$ (b) $s = \dfrac{a(r^n - 1)}{r - 1}$

   (c) $c = 2t^3 + \dfrac{72}{t^2}$ (d) $v = \dfrac{4}{3}\pi r^3$

4. You are now required to do some problem solving. The end result should be a simple Python program. You will be required to extract relevant information from the next paragraph, and write a program to compute the cost to fill the petrol tank from empty, the maximum distance on a full tank of fuel and the cost per mile.

   I have extracted from the technical specification of a Lexus RX450h the following information. It has a 3.5L V6 engine, with an official mileage efficiency of 43.5 miles per gallon (mpg) for urban travel. The fuel tank is 65 litres in size.

   At my local petrol station a litre of petrol costs £1.179. You can assume that there are 5.546 litres to the gallon.

Lesson 3: Strings

3.1 Introducing strings

We have previously seen strings. They have been described as a sequence of characters enclosed within quotes – either single, or double quotes. We will now be looking at strings in more detail

I can create a string variable by using an assignment statement.

The statement a = "hello" allocates storage sufficient to store the **literal string** "hello"; the literal string is then stored in this chunk of memory. In this case, the string is 5 characters in length. This can be represented diagrammatically as follows:

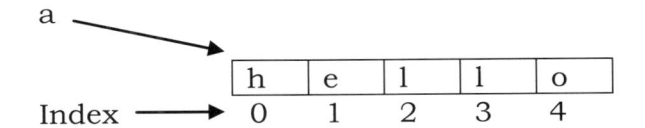

```
a ──────────┐
            ▼
          ┌───┬───┬───┬───┬───┐
          │ h │ e │ l │ l │ o │
          └───┴───┴───┴───┴───┘
Index ──▶   0   1   2   3   4
```

Here **a** points to the storage that contains the string. Each character within the string can be identified by an **index**. The index specifies the relative position of each character within the string. Note how the first character has index = 0.

We can test these ideas out using the Python shell.

```
>>> a = "hello"
>>> a[0]
'h'
>>> a[1]
'e'
>>> a[2]
'l'
>>> a[3]
'l'
>>> a[4]
'o'
>>>
```

Here I have used the **indexing operator** denoted using square bracket []. So, the expression a[0] denotes the character at position 0. You will notice that the index values for this string range from 0 to 4.

What would happen if I tried to access a[5]?

```
>>> a = "hello"
>>> a[5]
Traceback (most recent call last):
  File "<pyshell#1>", line 1, in <module>
    a[5]
IndexError: string index out of range
>>>
```

We have an error message indicating that we have entered an invalid index value. For this string, it must be the range 0 to 4.

Also, I do not need to use a variable to make use of the indexing operator. You can see this by looking at the example that follows.

```
>>> "hello"[0]
'h'
>>> "hello"[1]
'e'
>>> "hello"[2]
'l'
>>> "hello"[3]
'l'
>>> "hello"[4]
'o'
>>>
```

I now intend to say more about the indexing operator. It can be used to create what used to be called **sub-strings**. In Python speak, sub-strings are called **slices**.

```
>>> s = "abcdefghijklmnopqrstuvwxyz"
>>> s[0:3]
'abc'
>>> s[23:26]
'xyz'
>>> s[10:]
'klmnopqrstuvwxyz'
>>> s[:10]
'abcdefghij'
>>> s[10:13]
'klm'
>>>
```

The first example `s[0:3]` is the first 3 characters. It includes the characters `s[0]` to `s[2]`, but does not include `s[3]`.

The second example outputs characters determined by s[23] to s[25].

The third example outputs characters determined by s[10] to the end of the string.

The fourth example includes characters at the beginning of the string up to and including s[9]

The fifth example outputs the characters s[10] to s[12].

Each of the examples, are examples of what is called **string slicing**.

Another, rather simpler operator to use with strings is +. In the context of strings, this does not do addition in the arithmetic sense; it adds one string to the end of another string. This process is called **concatenation**.

```
>>> a = "Hello "
>>> b = "world!"
>>> a + b
'Hello world!'
>>>
```

In this example, I have created two strings, and then used the + (**concatenate**) operator to join them together. I could have stored the result in a variable by entering `c = a + b`. If I then entered c, I would obtain the same output.

I will now tall about another operator that is useful to see whether a substring is present in another string. This is the in operator.

```
>>> myName = "Tony Hawken"
>>> 'H' in myName
True
>>> 'Hawk' in myName
True
>>> 'x' in myName
False
>>>
```

The expression 'Tony' in myName searches the string myName, and returns True if it is found, False otherwise. You can use it for individual characters or any substring.

I will now talk about some properties of strings. Strings are said to be **immutable**. That is they cannot be changed. So, if I do the following in Python, I have in fact created two separate strings. But, only the second string can be accessed when both statements have been executed.

```
>>> name = "Tony"
>>> name
'Tony'
>>> name = "William"
>>> name
'William'
>>> name
'William'
>>>
```

Here you can see that the string variable intially refers to the string "Tony", then subsequently refers to the string "William".

This can be illustrated as follows:

Initially we have this.

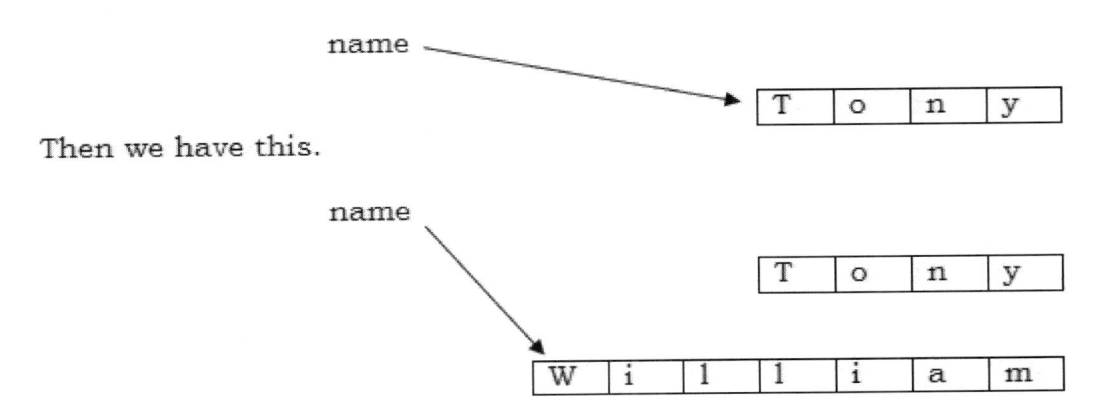

name → | T | o | n | y |

Then we have this.

name →

| T | o | n | y |

| W | i | l | l | i | a | m |

As you can see from my diagrams, the variable name now refers to the string "William". We now no longer have the means of accessing the string "Tony".

23

3.2 Special characters, and other things you can do with strings

Using a backslash (\) in front of certain characters creates a special character or escape sequence. These special characters allow us to display certain chacters that would otherwise be difficult to display.

```
>>> print("He said \"Hello there!\" ")
He said "Hello there!"
>>> print("\'Hello\'")
'Hello'
>>> print("This is a \\ character")
This is a \ character
>>>
```

The previous example demonstrates how you can display double quotes ("), single quotes (') and the backslash character (\).

In summary:

- The sequence \" is used to display double quotes
- The sequence \' is used to display single quotes
- The sequence \\ is used to display the backslash character

Even more useful, is the ability to represent carriage returns, and tabs. The following demonstrates this.

```
>>> print("abc\ndef\nghi\njkl")
abc
def
ghi
jkl
>>> print("a\tb\tc\td")
a       b       c       d
>>>
```

In the first example the sequence \n is used to perform a carriage return. That is the cursor moves to the next line before printing the next character.

In the second example, the sequence \t is used to include a tab. This moves the cursor one tab position to the right before printing the next character.

There are other escape sequences, but these are the only ones I choose to talk about.

Another useful feature, that to my knowledge does not appear in other programming languages, is the ability to repeat strings within a print statement.

```
>>> print("Hello" * 3)
HelloHelloHello
>>> print("Hello\t" * 4)
Hello   Hello   Hello   Hello
>>> print("Hello\n" * 3)
Hello
Hello
Hello

>>>
```

In the first example I am printing the string "Hello" 3 times. Here, the * operator in the context of strings is used to repeat the string a number of times, in this instance 3 times.

I have modified this statement to show the effect of using escape sequences in conjunction with the string repetition operator.

3.3 String functions and methods

So far, we have been talking about strings as if they are just a basic datatype within Python. They are in fact objects, as Python is an **object-oriented** language that deals with **classes** and **objects**. Strings belong to the **str** class.

So when I issue the command: `message = "Hello"`, I am creating a string object called message.

There are a number of string functions that can work on this. One of these is `len()`.

```
>>> message = "Hello, how are you?"
>>> len(message)
19
>>>
```

Here we have used the variable called message that refers to the string object. The function `len()` determines the number of characters in this string and returns this value.

```
>>> len("Hello")
5
>>>
```

As you can see, I do not have to use a variable as the parameter for len; I could use a literal instead.

Most of the other functions that form part of the string class are special functions called **methods**. These are distinguished from normal functions by the way that you call them. To use a string method you need a string object to call it.
Generally speaking, a method call takes the following format:

`stringObject.method()`

Here we use a dot notation to indicate a method call. In the above case, we say that the string object called `stringObject` calls the method called `method()`.

I will now include some examples, then explain what is happening.

```
>>> message = "Hello"
>>> message.upper()
'HELLO'
>>> message.lower()
'hello'
>>>
```

Here we can see that the string message calls the method called `upper()`. This converts the string to uppercase characters. The method `lower()` converts the string to lowercase characters.

I will now be looking at methods that test the nature of a string. They will return either True or False. Some examples follow which illustrate this.

```
>>> a = "ABCDEF"
>>> b = "abcdef"
>>> c = "ABCdef"
>>> d = "ABC123"
>>> e = "1234"
>>> f = "    "
>>> a.isupper()
True
>>> a.islower()
False
>>> b.isupper()
False
>>> b.islower()
True
>>> a.isalpha()
True
>>> b.isalnum()
True
>>> d.isalnum()
True
>>> e.isdigit()
True
>>> f.isspace()
True
>>> e.isalnum()
True
>>>
```

In this example session using the Python shell, the following methods are used.

1. `isupper()` returns True if all the characters in the string are uppercase, False otherwise.
2. `islower()` returns True if all the characters in the string are lowercase, False otherwise.
3. `isalpha()` returns True, if all the characters in the string are alphabetic, False otherwise.
4. `isalnum()` returns True, if all the characters in the string are alphanumeric, False otherwise. Alphanumeric means that they can either be alphabetic characters or numeric digits.
5. `isdigit()` returns True, if all the characters in the string are numeric digits, False otherwise.
6. `isspace()` returns True, if all the characters in the string are spaces, False otherwise.

3.4 Characters and their representation

All data is stored in the form of binary numbers. Characters are represented using small integers. The western alphabet that includes the characters on your keyboard and more besides, is represented using a coding scheme called ASCII. Each character is stored in 1 byte of storage is made up of 8 binary digits (bits). Altogether there are $2^8 = 256$ different combinations, so you can represent 256 different characters.

So, each character that is represented has its own ASCII code. You can determine what that is using the `ord()` function. The name `ord` is short for **ordinal number**. An ordinal number denotes the position of the character within the ASCII table.

```
>>> ord('A')
65
>>> ord('a')
97
>>>
```

You will notice the lowercase letters have a higher ASCII code than uppercase characters.

There is also a function that returns a character given the ASCII code.

```
>>> chr(65)
'A'
>>> chr(98)
'b'
>>> chr(10)
'\n'
>>>
```

The last example here returns the carriage-return, or new line character.

3.5 A programming problem using strings

Suppose I want to create a simple box using the characters you can find on the keyboard. Then inside this box I want to display one or more strings.

I will be making use of the repetition operator for strings (*). I will start by experimenting as follows.

```
>>> c1 = '+'
>>> c2 = '-'
>>> c3 = '|'
>>> c4 = ' '
>>> c1 + c2 * 18 + c1
'+------------------+'
>>> c3 + c4 * 18 + c3
'|                  |'
>>>
```

You can see from the above, that I have created new strings using a combination of concatenation, and also by using the repetition operator. In the first case, I have used a plus sign, followed by 18 minus signs, followed by another plus sign.

The tricky part of the problem is fitting a string inside the box. To do this I will also need to use the `len()` function to determine the number of characters in the strings I want to insert.

Suppose one of my strings is `s1 = 'Programming with'`. I can determine the number of characters in this string with the function call `len(s1)`. So, if I want to calculate the number of spaces I need, I can calculate this by subtracting this value away from the number of spaces I have left.

The completed program is as follows:

```
# Draw a box with a couple of strings in it

# characters for box
c1 = '+'
c2 = '-'
c3 = '|'
c4 = ' '
# Strings to insert
s1 = 'Programming with'
s2 = 'Python is easy'

# print box
print(c1 + c2 * 18 + c1)
print(c3 + c4 * 18 + c3)
print(c3 + c4 + s1 + c4 * (17 - len(s1)) + c3)
print(c3 + c4 + s2 + c4 * (17 - len(s2)) + c3)
print(c3 + c4 * 18 + c3)
print(c1 + c2 * 18 + c1)
```

And the output from this program is:

```
+------------------+
|                  |
| Programming with |
| Python is easy   |
|                  |
+------------------+
>>>
```

Exercise 3

1. Given the string s1 = 'Python programming is easy'; determine the values of the following expressions:

   (a) `s1[4]`   (b) `s1[16:23]`   (c) `s[8] + s[4] + s[13]`

   (d) `len(s1)`   (e) `len(s1[16:23])` (f) `s1[23:]`

   (g) `s1[16:23].upper()`   (h) `s1[6].isspace()`

2. Write a program that will produce a horizontal bar chart using instances of the character * to represent the frequency. Use the following data. Suggested output has also been given.

Radio station	Number of listeners	Radio station	Number of listeners
Radio 1	7	Radio 1	*******
Radio 2	4	Radio 2	****
Radio 4	5	Radio 4	*****
Radio X	18	Radio X	******************
		>>>	

Lesson 4: More about data types in Python

4.1 Introduction to data types continued

If you read a GCSE (9-1) Computer Science syllabus, it typically has the following expectations.

Students should have studied the following about **data types**. This includes a knowledge and use of integers, real numbers, characters and strings, and the Boolean type. Also, knowledge about casting.

I have already had something to say about integers, real numbers and strings. I will start by stating that Python does not have a separate character data type. It does have strings. A string is a self-contained sequence of characters. The nearest you get to a character in Python is a string of length 1. So, the following can be treated as characters, even though Python treats them as strings.

a = 'a'   This is a string that contains the character a.

b = chr(98)   This is a string that contains the character that has an ASCII code of 98. In this case b.

You can check a variables type using the `type()` function.

```
>>> h = 'hello'
>>> a = 'a'
>>> b = chr(98)
>>> type(h)
<class 'str'>
>>> type(a)
<class 'str'>
>>> type(b)
<class 'str'>
>>> c = ord(b)
>>> type(c)
<class 'int'>
>>>
```

The class `str` is the class that defines strings. This class contains information about the string data type and the methods that can be called by string objects. So, if you use a `type()` function and it returns `<class 'str'>`, you know you have a string.

So, we know that 'a' and 'b' are also strings, even though they consist of a single character.

We can see that the variable c is an integer because the type statement returns:

`<class 'int'>`

Remember, the `ord()` function takes a character string as a parameter, and returns an integer that corresponds to the ASCII code.

In a similar way we can use the `type()` function to test other values such as real numbers and Booleans. For the moment, I will just say that a Boolean variable can have one of two values, `True`, or `False`.

The following gives a simple illustration of the main types in Python.

```
>>> a = 'a'
>>> b = 2
>>> c = 2.75
>>> d = True
>>> type(a)
<class 'str'>
>>> type(b)
<class 'int'>
>>> type(c)
<class 'float'>
>>> type(d)
<class 'bool'>
>>>
```

The second example returns a value of <class 'int'> . The class int is the class that deals with integers. So, if you see 'int' you know you have an integer or whole number.

The third is a float or floating point number. A float is an approximation to what we call a real number in mathematics. As far as you are concerned, a float is a number with a decimal point in it.

The fourth return value refers to the class `bool`. This class specifies a data type called a Boolean. It can have one of two values, True, False, or a numerical equivalent. It was named after a 19th century mathematician called George Boole. He was responsible for the creation of a system of symbolic logic that is now called Boolean algebra.

4.2 The data type Boolean and relational operators.

As, I have already stated, a Boolean variable typically can only store one of two values, `True` or `False`. The values `True`, and `False` are **literal Boolean constants**. They can be used to tell us whether a logical expression is true or false.

A **Boolean** (logical) expression always evaluates to **True** or **False**. Later on, we will see much more use of logical expressions and Booleans. They will be used in statements for carrying out **selection**, and also for statements for **repetition**. The relational operators are shown in a table below.

Mathematical operation	Python operation	meaning
a = b	a == b	a has same value as b
a < b	a < b	a is less than b
a ≤ b	a <= b	a is less than or equal to b
a > b	a > b	a is greater than b
a ≥ b	a >= b	a is greater than or equal to b
a ≠ b	a != b	a is not equal to b

We can test these expressions provided we have some values for a and b. By forming an expression, such as the ones in the previous table, we have an expression that can either be true of false. For this reason they are often called Boolean expressions.

Below I have a screen dump of a session using the Python shell.

```
>>> a = 2
>>> b = 5
>>> a == b
False
>>> a < b
True
>>> a <= b
True
>>> a > b
False
>>> a >= b
False
>>> a != b
True
>>>
```

Given that a = 2, and b = 3, you could have worked out the truth value of these Boolean expressions yourself.

I could have done exactly the same thing with floats. So, if this time I had changed a to 2.0 and b to 3.0, I would have obtained exactly the same results.

These Boolean expressions can also be used with different data types. An example follows.

```
>>> a = 2
>>> type(a)
<class 'int'>
>>> b = 2.0
>>> type(b)
<class 'float'>
>>> a == b
True
>>>
```

What does this show? It tells me that the integer 2 is equivalent in value to the float 2.0.

You can also use these relational operators for string comparisons. The order of two characters is determined by the relative value of their ASCII code. Roughly speaking the purpose of performing string comparison is to order strings according to alphabetical order. This of course will work provided that only alphabetic characters of the same case are used in the strings.

In the ASCII table we have:

Description of character	character	ASCII code
Numeric characters	0 - 9	48 - 57
Uppercase characters	A - Z	65 - 90
Lowercase characters	a - z	97 - 122

As well as punctuation characters, various non-printing characters and also some graphics characters are present.

So we could write the following valid expressions:

$$\text{"a"} < \text{"b"}$$

$$\text{"Z"} < \text{"a"}$$

$$\text{"4"} < \text{"6"}$$

This can be verified by checking the ASCII codes for each character in question. When I am talking about characters, I am of course referring to strings that have length = 1.

If we use two longer strings, strings are ordered by comparing their characters one at a time until there is a mismatch. Consider the following:

"business" < "busy"

This can be represented as:

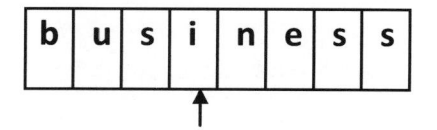

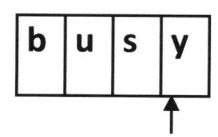

b	u	s	i	n	e	s	s
           ↑

b	u	s	y
           ↑

Here the first mismatch is at 4th character position, indicating that "business" < "busy", because the letter i comes before y in the ASCII table. In the same way if we consider the comparison of:

"word" < "words"

This would evaluate true because the first mismatch would be detected on the fifth character, making this expression true. This is because the first string only has 4 characters, and the second has more.

We can also use all of the other relational operators to compare two strings.

Below, I have considered comparing two strings. If I want them in alphabetical order I must make sure they have the same case. In this instance, I only needed to convert string b to lower case. Now I get the correct answer, assuming I wanted the words in alphabetical order.

```
>>> a = "business"
>>> b = "BUSY"
>>> a < b
False
>>> b = b.lower()
>>> a < b
True
>>>
```

4.3 Logical connectives and truth tables

The unary operator **not** is used to negate an expression. That is, an expression whose value is **True** will become **False** and vice versa.

If I start with the expression a < b and it has been determined that this has a value True, then `not(a < b)` must necessarily be False. This process is often called **negation.**

The logical operators **and** and **or** are used to combine simple logical expressions to form more complex ones. Here is an example.

$$(x > 5) \quad \text{and} \quad (x < 20)$$

An expression formed with the **and** operator like the one above will only evaluate **True** if both of the simpler conditions are **True**. In the example above we are testing whether the value of x is in the range 5 to 20.

i.e. 5 < x < 20

The logical operator **or** when used to combine two expressions will evaluate **True** if either or both of the expressions are **True**.

The expression `(x > 5) or (y == 0)` is interpreted as **True** if either of the expressions or both evaluate **True**.

For your clarification I have included truth tables of the operators **and**, **or** and **not**. These summarize what I have previously stated.

and

x	y	x and y
F	F	F
T	F	F
F	T	F
T	T	T

or

x	y	x or y
F	F	F
T	F	T
F	T	T
T	T	T

not

x	not(x)
F	T
T	F

Truth tables were first used by Ludwig Wittgenstein. They appear in his book Tractatus Logico-Philosopicus (TLP). This was first published in German in 1921.

4.4 Type casting

Type casting is the process of converting one data type to another type. Besides Python, it is also present in other programming languages such as C++. It makes more sense to call this type conversion.

You get type conversion done automatically when you evaluate certain arithmetic expressions. Consider the following.

```
>>> a = 2
>>> b = 2.4
>>> c = a + b
>>> type(c)
<class 'float'>
>>>
```

Here we are doing a calculation that involves an integer and a float. With a mixed type operation like this the result is always converted to a float. That is why variable c is a float.

This one is not quite so obvious.

```
>>> c = 25
>>> f = 9 / 5 * c + 32
>>> type(f)
<class 'float'>
>>> f
77.0
>>>
```

Why is f a float? This is to do with the real division operator /. You will recall that whenever you perform real division, the result is a float. It just happens that the value of f is 77.0 which is equivalent to 77. Also, part of the operation carried out is 9/5. This is equivalent to 1.8 (a float). But if you multiply by the value of c (25), you get 45.0 and not 45. Had we worked this out on paper, we would never have obtained a float, because we would cancel the 5 with 25.

There are situations where you need to force the conversion. This is called **forced conversion** or **explicit casting**.

```
>>> a = 2
>>> b = float(a)
>>> type(b)
<class 'float'>
>>> b
2.0
>>>
```

In this example, the integer 2 has been converted to the float 2.0. The function `float()` takes the integer value 2 and returns the floating point number 2.0.

If I were to be pedantic, I would say that `float()` was a constructor within the float class. This constructor takes an integer parameter of 2 in this instance, and constructs a floating point number with a value of 2.0. This is an object-oriented explanation; you are not required to know or understand this.

You can also convert a floating point number to an integer.

```
>>> a = 2.5
>>> b = int(a)
>>> type(b)
<class 'int'>
>>> b
2
>>>
```

In this case, to convert a float to an integer, the number needs to be truncated. That is, all of the number after the decimal point is removed.

Strings can also be converted to numbers with a cast, provided all of the characters are appropriate numeric digits.

The next example converts a string to an integer.

```
>>> s = "2"
>>> t = int(s)
>>> type(t)
<class 'int'>
>>> t
2
>>>
```

This one converts a string to a floating point number.

```
>>> s = "2.5"
>>> t = float(s)
>>> type(t)
<class 'float'>
>>> t
2.5
>>>
```

Remember, to convert a string to an integer, all of the characters must be the numeric digits 0 to 9. If the string is to be converted to a float, exactly one of the digits must be a decimal point, and the others must be numeric digits.

You can also convert integers, and floats to strings.

```
>>> a = 32
>>> b = str(a)
>>> b
'32'
>>> type(b)
<class 'str'>
>>> c = 2.65
>>> d = str(c)
>>> d
'2.65'
>>> type(d)
<class 'str'>
>>>
```

The constructor `str()` from the str class in the first example takes the integer value 32 as a parameter and creates the string '32'. In the second example, the constructor `str()` takes the floating point value 2.65 as a parameter and creates the string '2.65'.

It may seem perverse, but you can also cast Booleans to integers.

```
>>> int(False)
0
>>> int(True)
1
>>>
```

Here we can see that 0 and 1 can also valid Boolean types. We could if we like, use the `bool()` constructor to change them back to a Boolean data type.

Exercise 4

1. Evaluate the following Boolean expressions.

   (a)   5 == 7   (e)   (15 > 5) and (7 == 0)

   (b)   9 <= 9   (f)   not (15 > 5) or (7 == 0)

   (c)   11 > (14 - 5)   (g)   not (15 > 5) or (7 = 0)

   (d)   (15 > 5) or (7 = 0)   (h)   not ((15 > 5) and (7 = 0))

2. What are the types of the following expressions:

   (a)   False and True   (b)   False or True

   (c)   False + True   (d)   True and (False or True)

   (e)   8 / 2 + 4   (f)   2 * 2 ** 4 + 3.0

   (g)   (4 + 6) // 2   (h)   (4 + 6) % 4

Remember you can use the Python shell to check out your answers.

Lesson 5: Keyboard input, output, and sequence

5.1 Introduction to sequential programming

A typical (9-1) computer science syllabus will state that students will have studied the use of the three basic programming constructs used to control the flow of a program. These include: sequence, selection, and iteration.

In the context of structured procedural programming, many believe that there are only three programming constructs with which you can write any program.

1. **Sequence**

Here program statements follow one after the other. They are executed starting at the top of the program (beginning), moving onto the next statement below, and so on until the bottom of the program is reached (end).

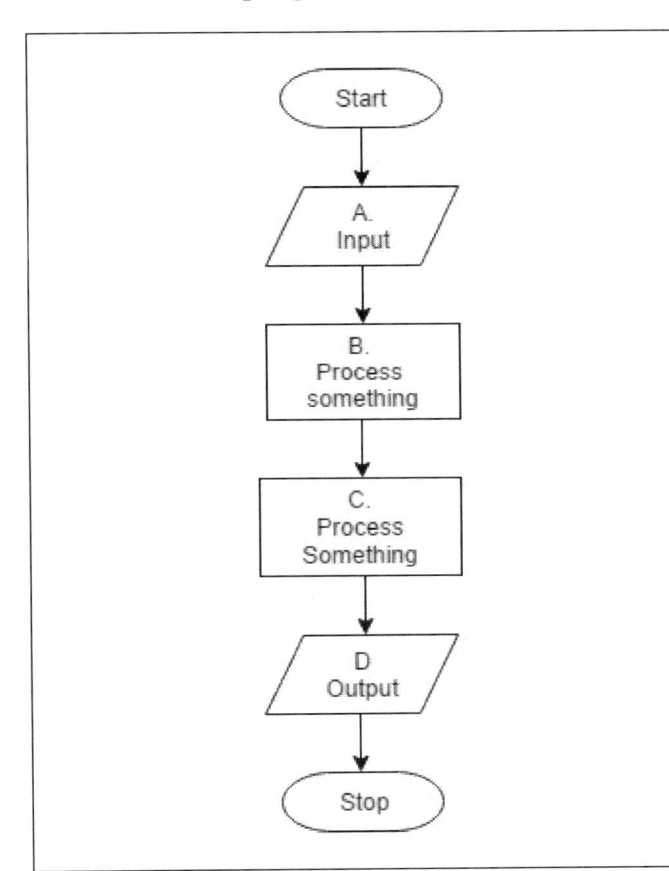

Start → A. Input → B. Process something → C. Process Something → D. Output → Stop	The flow chart on the left illustrates a sequence. The program starts at the top, then, proceeds to the next statement as indicated by the arrows.
	The rounded rectangles are traditionally used for start and stop.
	The parallelograms are used for input and output.
	The rectangular boxes are used for processes. A process can be any form of computation. It may be calculating an arithmetic expression and then assigning the value to a variable.
	In this case, the statements are run in the order A, B, C, and D. This is what is meant by a sequence in the context of procedural programming.

In very simple terms, a sequence is about putting the program statements in the correct order. For instance you cannot perform a calculation, unless you have values for the variables on the right-hand-side of the expression. The same goes for output. You need to have worked out all of the results required by the print statement, before you can execute the print statement.

2. **Selection**

Selection provides a choice. You are able to execute a certain statement, or an alternative. Which one you execute is determined by the results of a test.

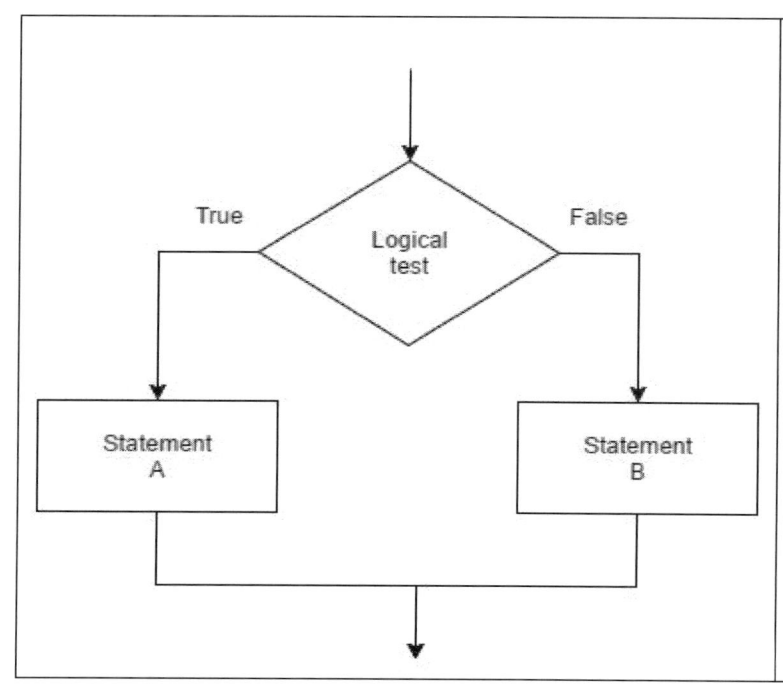

(flow chart: Logical test diamond with True → Statement A, False → Statement B, merging to a single output)	The flow chart on the left illustrates a selection. The diamond shape contains a condition that is tested. This typically results in a value of true or false. The value returned will determine which of the statements will be executed. The statement A will be executed if True, B otherwise.

3. **Iteration**

Iteration is a fancy word for repetition. A section of code can be repeated many times.

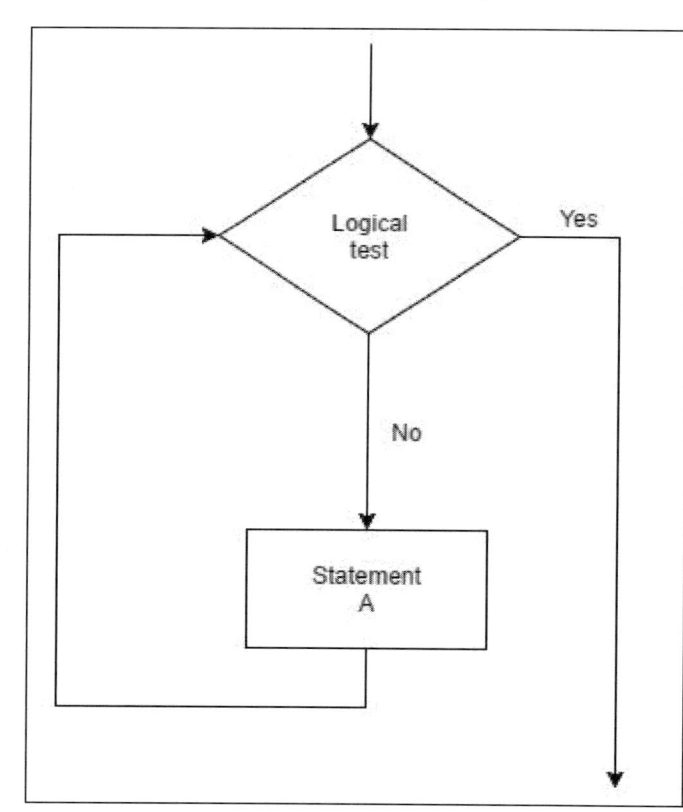

(flow chart: Logical test diamond with Yes exiting loop, No going to Statement A, which loops back to the Logical test)	The start of the loop in this flow chart is a diamond. Here a decision is made which will determine whether the repetition will be terminated. If the terminating condition has not been met, Statement A will be continue to be executed. Statement A can be repeated many times. If the termination condition has been met, statement A is no longer executes. Instead control of the program bypasses this loop, and continues to the next part of the program.

These three structures are claimed to be the basis of structured programming. The idea was put forward by Bohm and Jacopini in 1966. They demonstrated that any flowchart could be represented using only these three structures. It was a means to eliminate the dreaded goto statements from all programming.

A computer program can be thought to consist of 3 different components:

Input, Processing and Output

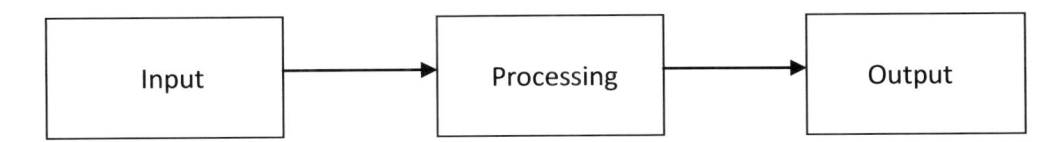

```
[Input] → [Processing] → [Output]
```

Input is the action of transferring data from an external device such as a keyboard or mouse to locations in main-memory. In Python, I will be using the `input()` function to obtain input from the keyboard.

Output is the action of transferring data from main-memory to an external device such as a screen or printer. For the moment, I will continue using the `print()` function.

Processing is the term used here to describe the operations on data in main-memory. This would include assignment statements that perform calculations.

Some or all of these components must be present in a program. Although it must be admitted that a program with no output would be rather pointless as it would be rather difficult to verify that it had in fact worked.

5.2 Keyboard input

We will be using the `input()` function to provide us with user input from the keyboard. The simplest example follows.

```
>>> a = input()
|
```

This statement is supposed to take the input from the keyboard, and store the result in the variable a. The problem is, I have not been told to type anything in. That is why the cursor is on the next line waiting for input.

```
>>> a = input()
2
>>> a
'2'
>>> |
```

I have now type in a value of 2. I have typed a, to check the value of the keyboard input.

I need a prompt to tell me what to do. I could include a print statement just before the input statement to achieve this. However, I do not need to do this. The `input()` function is able to accept a string as a parameter. This string supplies the prompt.

```
>>> name = input("Enter your name ")
Enter your name Tony
>>> name
'Tony'
>>>
```

This time when I run the input statement, I obtain a prompt that indicates what I should be typing. You will notice that all keyboard input using the `input()` function is a string. That could be a problem if I want to input numbers. However I can do an explicit type conversion to solve this problem.

```
>>> number = input("Enter a whole number ")
Enter a whole number 5
>>> number
'5'
>>> number = int(number)
>>> number
5
>>>
```

Here you can see that the initial input was the string '5', I have then used the `int()` function to convert this string to an integer.

Alternatively, I could have used the statement:

```
number = int(input("Enter a whole number "))
```

Here I am converting the input data to an integer directly. If you do it this way, make sure that your left and right brackets match up.

The inclusion of keyboard input from the user allows us to make our programs more general. If we return to an earlier program to convert temperatures from degrees Centigrade to degrees Fahrenheit, rather than just have a fixed value, the user can select a value for the temperature in degrees centigrade. Below, I have a program written in script mode.

```
# Convert degrees Centigrade to Fahrenheit

c = int(input("Enter a temperature in degrees C "))
f = 9 /5 * c + 32
print("The temperature in Fahrenheit is ", f)
```

When I run this and input a value of 25, I obtain the following.

```
Enter a temperature in degrees C 25
The temperature in Fahrenheit is  77.0
>>>
```

I can of course run this program again, but input a different value.

5.3 Another programming problem with keyboard input

A quadratic equation is of the form: $ax^2 + bx + c = 0$. It can be shown that there is a general formula as follows.

$$x = \frac{-b \pm \sqrt{b^2 - 4ac}}{2a}$$

As it is a quadratic, there will be two solutions.

$$x1 = \frac{-b + \sqrt{b^2 - 4ac}}{2a} \quad \text{and} \quad x2 = \frac{-b - \sqrt{b^2 - 4ac}}{2a}$$

We can code these statements in Python as follows.

```
x1 = (- b + math.sqrt(b ** 2 - 4 * a * c) / (2 * a)

x2 = (- b - math.sqrt(b ** 2 - 4 * a * c) / (2 * a)
```

Notice there is a lot of duplication in these statements. The computation would be more efficient if I were to calculate the discriminant separately beforehand.

The discriminant is a mathematical term to describe the expression $b^2 - 4ac$.

My calculation below now has 3 steps. But you will notice that this actually simplifies my code.

```
d = math.sqrt(b ** 2 - 4 * a * c)

x1 = (-b + d) / (2 * a)

x2 = (-b - d) / (2 * a)
```

In this case the variable d refers to the square root of the discriminant. This can be used to obtain the roots of the quadratic equation: x1, and x2,

To complete the program, I need to include some input statements to obtain values for the coefficients a, b, and c. I also need a print statement to output the results. The completed program follows.

```
# Compute roots of a quadratic equation
import math

a = int(input("Enter coefficient for a "))
b = int(input("Enter coefficient for b "))
c = int(input("Enter coefficient for c "))

d = math.sqrt(b ** 2 - 4 * a * c)
x1 = (-b + d) / (2 * a)
x2 = (-b - d) / (2 * a)

print("The roots are ", x1, " and ", x2)
```

And, some sample runs follow.

```
Enter coefficient for a 2
Enter coefficient for b 5
Enter coefficient for c 3
The roots are   -1.0   and   -1.5
>>>
```

In this case, I was lucky. My results work out to 2 decimal places.

```
Enter coefficient for a 2
Enter coefficient for b 3
Enter coefficient for c -7
The roots are  1.2655644370746373  and  -2.7655644370746373
>>>
```

In the second run, I did not obtain nice looking results. I would really like the numbers rounded to 2 decimal places.

The easiest way to do this is to use the mathematics function `round()`.

Before I modify the program I will test out `round()`.

```
>>> a = 4.47291
>>> round(a)
4
>>> round(a, 1)
4.5
>>> round(a, 2)
4.47
>>> round(a, 3)
4.473
>>>
```

The first example, rounds to the nearest whole number. The second rounds to 1 decimal place and the third to 2 decimal places etc.

I could improve the appearance of the output of the program by replacing the current print statement with the following.

`print("The roots are ", round(x1, 2), " and ", round(x2, 2))`

There are situations where the program will fail. The following program run has generated a run-time error.

```
Enter coefficient for a 2
Enter coefficient for b 3
Enter coefficient for c 4
Traceback (most recent call last):
  File "C:\Documents and Settings\Admin\Desktop\My Python programs\quad.py", line 8, in <module>
    d = math.sqrt(b ** 2 - 4 * a * c)
ValueError: math domain error
>>>
```

The interpreter has detected an error while trying to execute the statement to compute d.

Let's do some maths, and see what the problem is.

If we were to calculate $b^2 - 4ac$ given that a = 2, b = 3, c = 4

This is $3^2 - 4 \times 2 \times 4 = 9 - 32 = -23$

The problem is calculating the square root of a negative number is forbidden. You can test this in you calculator. You will get Math ERROR or something similar.

We really need to avoid such situations, but we will have to wait until a later lesson to do this.

5.4 Problem solving

Problem solving is an important part of programming. Sometimes you have to solve problems that you have never seen before. Some people would say that you should start by writing down an algorithm on paper, possibly in the form of **pseudo-code**. Pseudo-code is a description of the problem in a language that describes what has to be done, but must be language-independent. If you are studying OCR computer science, the pseudo-code in places too closely resembles Python.

I would encourage you to write down rough ideas on paper, and then test them out using the Python interactive shell. Only then proceed with an algorithm.

Statement of problem

Write a program to work out a person's change. It is assumed that the item costs less than £10 and that the person only has a £10 note to pay with. The required change should then be calculated so that a minimum number of coins are given. No notes are given as change.

Analysis of problem

1. Easier if change is converted to pence.
2. Coins currently available are £2, £1, 50p, 20p, 10p, 5p, 2p, 1p.
3. Need to keep a coin count for each coin.
4. Can use the built-in arithmetic operators // and %.

At this stage it is a good idea to try things out using the interactive shell. Suppose the change that is to be given is £3.64. This is equivalent to 364p. We can obtain this figure by multiplying 3.64 by 100. The number of pounds can be obtained by using the integer division operator //.

That is `pounds = change // 100`.

The remainder, when you have subtracted the amount in pounds will be `change % 100`.

The following is a session using the Python interactive shell.

```
>>> change = 364
>>> pounds = change // 100
>>> pounds
3
>>> remainder = change % 100
>>> remainder
64
>>> fifty = remainder // 50
>>> fifty
1
>>> remainder = remainder % 50
>>> remainder
14
>>>
```

You can see that this is working as expected.

Now I want to describe an algorithm. I could use pseudo-code. If you are going to do this, you need to check out the form of the pseudo-code for you exam board. My pseudo code goes like this. This is my version of pseudo-code; you possibly won't find it anywhere else. I just made it up, but it makes sense to me.

Pseudo-code

Input cost of item in pounds
Convert cost in pounds to pence: cost = cost * 100
Calculate change: change = 1000 – cost
Calculate number of pound coins: pounds = change // 100
Calculate amount left over: remainder = change % 100
Calculate number of 50p coins: fifty = remainder
Calculate amount left over: remainder = remainder % 50
You follow the same pattern for 20p, 10p, 5p, 2p coins.
I will let you work this out
Number of penny coins = remainder
Print out number of coins: print(pounds, fifty, twenty, ten, five, two, one)

The full program is appears on the next page. I had to make a few changes at the last minute. In particular I needed to convert the coin counts to an integer. It makes no sense having the coin count values as a floating point number. Also, to improve the appearance of the output, I had to include tabs in the last two print statements. This is achieved using the escape sequence \t.

```
# Program to calculate change and number of each coin

note = 10        # Ten pound note
cost = float(input("Enter amount in pounds "))
change = 100 * note - 100 * cost

pounds = int(change // 100)
remainder = change % 100
fifty = int(remainder // 50)
remainder = remainder % 50
twenty = int(remainder // 20)
remainder = remainder % 20
ten = int(remainder // 10)
remainder = remainder % 10
five = int(remainder // 5)
remainder = remainder % 5
two = int(remainder // 2)
remainder = remainder % 2
one = int(remainder)
# Convert change back into pounds
change = change / 100

print("change is £", change)
print("£\t50p\t20p\t10p\t5p\t2p\t1p")
print(pounds, '\t', fifty, '\t', twenty, '\t', ten, '\t',five,'\t', two,'\t', one)
```

I tested the program with the cost of £3.64.

```
Enter amount in pounds 3.64
change is £ 6.36
£       50p     20p     10p     5p      2p      1p
6       0       1       1       1       0       1
>>>
```

At this stage of programming, you do not have to be too fussy with the format of your algorithm. You are not doing a piece of coursework yet. The most important thing is to find a system that works for you.

Exercise 5

1. Write a program that will:

    (a) allow a user to enter their Name, Address and Telephone number.

    (b) print out the name, address and telephone number just entered.

2. The formula $gasMark = \frac{F-275}{25} + 1$ gives an approximate conversion from degrees Fahrenheit to the British Gas mark on a cooker for temperatures between 275 and 1000 degrees F.

    Write a short program that will:

    (a) allow a user to enter a temperature in Fahrenheit that is between 275 and 1000.

    (b) compute the Gas mark and print out the result in an appropriate format.

    (c) include appropriate comments to make the program readable.

Lesson 6: Selection - making a choice

6.1 Selection using the if statement

We often want the execution of a statement to depend on whether a condition is true or false. That is, if the condition is true, we execute the statement that follows, otherwise we do nothing. This is achieved using a conditional statement such as an **if** statement. In the context of structured programming, this is called **selection**.

In Python, the simplest format of the **if** statement is:

```
if <boolean expression> :
    <statement>
```

Where <Boolean expression>, can be replaced by a Boolean expression, either simple or compound. And, <statement> can be one or more statements that we would want to be executed.

This is to be interpreted as, if the expression is true execute the statements, otherwise do nothing.

e.g.
```
if num > 0 :
    print("num is positive")
```

I now want to comment about the Python syntax in more detail. Firstly, it is important to include a colon (:) after the Boolean expression. This colon, indicates that one or more statements will follow, and that these statements are the ones to be executed if the Boolean expression evaluates true.

Another feature of Python is that these statements have to be indented. All the indented statements are then identified as belonging to the same block of code. In other languages such as C++ it is normal to identify a block of code by containing it within curly brackets.

Using C++ I would write:

```
if (num > 0)
    cout << "Num is positive";
```

And, if I had two statements to execute following the Boolean test, I would write:

```
if (num > 0)
{
    numPositive = true;
    cout << "num is positive";
}
```

The equivalent code in Python would be:

```
if num > 0 :
    numPositive = True
    print("num is positive")
```

So, these two statements represent a code block. Both statements are executed if the condition num > 0 is true. Indentation in most languages including C++ is optional. People generally indent code to make it more readable. In the case of the Python language, you have to indent your code appropriately, otherwise it will not work properly. So, Python forces you to indent code. A by-product of this is the fact that your code is more readable.

When the `if` statement and associated block of statements comes to an end, it is essential that you remove this indentation for the next statement in your program code.

The if statement can be extended to provide an action if the expression evaluates false.

```
e.g.   if num > 0 :
           print("positive")
       else :
           print("non-positive")
```

Generally speaking the `if` ... `else` construct as shown above has the following format:

```
if (<boolean expression>) :
    <statement 1>
else :
    <statement 2>
```

This is interpreted as: Evaluate the Boolean expression. If it is true, execute statement 1, otherwise execute statement 2. Note in place of <statement 1> and <statement 2>, I could have had several statements.

This example can be taken a stage further. After all if we are going to classify numbers we might want to say they are negative, positive, or zero. The following code shows this.

```
if (num < 0 ):
    print("negative")
elif : (num > 0):
    print("positive")
else :
    print("ZERO")
```

In this case, we have used the keyword `elif`. This enables us to perform another test. If the result of this test is true, then the statements, or block of statements that follow, are executed.

The else clause is only ever executed if both of the previous two tests return False.

Note, also it is possible to have as many `elif` clauses as we like. This is called a multi-way selection statement, and sometimes a case structure. Some programming languages have such a case statement to implement a multi-way selection. C++ does, but it is not very useful, and programmers rarely use it. Python has no such statement.

A complete program follows.

```python
# Test nature of an integer - positive, negative, or zero

num = int(input("Enter an integer: "))

if num < 0 :
    print("number is negative")
elif num > 0 :
    print("number is positive")
else :
    print("number is zero")
```

6.2 Quadratic equations revisited

You will recall that we previously wrote a program to compute the roots of a quadratic equation. There were many circumstances when this program would fail. Instead of giving us a result, we would obtain an error message instead.

The problem we encountered was the fact that we tried to calculate the square root of a negative number. This problem arises when the discriminant of the equation is less than zero. That is, $b^2 - 4ac < 0$. In this situation, we say the equation has no real roots. When this happens, we need to print a message to indicate that the equation has no real roots instead of trying to calculate the square root of the discriminant.

The finished program follows.

```python
# Compute roots of a quadratic equation
import math

a = int(input("Enter coefficient for a "))
b = int(input("Enter coefficient for b "))
c = int(input("Enter coefficient for c "))

d = b ** 2 - 4 * a * c

if d >= 0 :
    d = math.sqrt(d)
    x1 = (-b + d) / (2 * a)
    x2 = (-b - d) / (2 * a)
    print("The roots are ", round(x1, 2), " and ", round(x2, 2))
else :
    print("Equation has no real roots")
```

You will notice that initially, my variable d is assigned to b ** 2 − 4 * a * c. I can now test the value of d to see if it is positive. If it is, I can work out the square root. If not, I print a message indicating that there are no real roots.

You will notice that I have also modified the print statement that displays the roots x1 and x2. I have used the round function, to round the values of x1 and x2 to 2 decimal places. A sample output that demonstrates this follows.

```
Enter coefficient for a 3
Enter coefficient for b 7
Enter coefficient for c 4
The roots are   -1.0   and   -1.33
>>>
```

Below, there is sample output of what you get when there are no real roots.

```
Enter coefficient for a 2
Enter coefficient for b 3
Enter coefficient for c 5
Equation has no real roots
>>>
```

6.3 Validation and verification

In this section we will be looking at ways to check whether data that has been input is reasonable. We will be looking at two methods – validation and verification.

Validation is the checking of data to see whether it is reasonable. It can only detect whether the data entered is obviously wrong. I cannot detect that the data is correct.

For instance, if someone is applying for a driving license, you may want to check that they are old enough. At the other extreme, you don't want people who are too old.

In this situation, you may assume that the age range will be given by the following:

$17 \leq age \leq 80$

What I have described is a range of possible values. Validation that checks to see whether data falls within a certain range is called a **range check**.

Another way of describing this range is to say age $\geq$ 17 and age $\leq$ 80. We can code this directly into Python as follows:

```
if age >= 17 and age <= 80 :
    print("This is a valid age")
else :
    print("Age entered is out of range")
```

Some people would code this using a nested if statement as follows:

```
if age >= 17 :
    if age <= 80 :
        print("This is a valid age")
else:
    print("Age entered is out of range")
```

I have done this, just to show you that this is possible. In this case, the first logical test is to determine the truth value of age >= 17. If this is true you are then presented with another test. If age <= 80 is also true, "This is a valid age" is printed out. If it is the case, that one or more of these conditions are false, "Age entered is out of range" is printed instead.

Although this is possible, I urge you not to do it. It is very bad programming practice, as it makes the logic of the if statement more difficult to understand.

The next example uses a string. Sometimes when you enter a string, it must be less than a certain length.

I have included a completed program below which we can discuss.

```
name = input("Enter name - maximum 10 characters ")

if len(name) > 10 :
    print("Name is too long")
    print("It will be truncated")
    name = name[:10]
else :
    print("Name entered is valid")

print("value of name is ", name)
```

In this example, the if statement is very simple. We use the `len()` function to determine the size of the string. This value is used to determine whether the string is too long. If it is too long it is truncated by doing a string slice. Only the 10 left-most characters are stored in name.

```
Enter name - maximum 10 characters Encyclopaedia
Name is too long
It will be truncated
value of name is  Encyclopae
>>>
```

Another type validation involves checking that data input is in the correct format. So, you may be asked to enter a date of birth in the format dd/mm/yyyy.

Here the characters dd indicate two numeric digits for the day, mm indicates two numeric digits for the month, and yyyy indicates four numeric digits for the year. This is another problem that can make use of string slices.

Verification is another method for checking input data. This time when data is entered, the user may be asked to indicate whether this is correct by doing a visual inspection. Alternatively, a very common method is to enter the data again. This is the typical method used if you register for an online account and have to enter a password for the first time. At no time is there a check to see whether the data is valid.

An example of verification follows.

```
pwd1 = input("Enter your password ")
pwd2 = input("Re-enter your password ")

if pwd1 == pwd2 :
    print("Password has passed verification check")
    pwd = pwd1
else :
    print("Verification failed")
    print("Password has not been changed")
```

The if statement here involves a simple comparison to see that the same password has been entered both times.

6.4 Problem solving: Days in a month

The following problem represents a more realistic and difficult problem to solve. As you will see, it involves a number of if statements in the program. And, one of these statements is quite complex.

Specification

(a) Write a program that will accept a given year. The program will then determine whether this year is a leap year and print an appropriate message. You may consider using the following rules for determining leap years.

Hint

To be a leap year, the year is divisible by 4 but not by 100, or the year is divisible by 4 and by 400.

(b) Continue this program by allowing a user to enter a number between 1 and 12 that represents a month. Given this number that represents the month and the fact that the year is a leap year or not a leap year, work out how many days in the month.

For part (a), it is first necessary to understand what the hint means. There are two conditions and one or more of them must be true for it to be a leap-year.

The first condition can be written as: year % 4 == 0 and year % 100 != 0.

The expression: `year % 4 == 0` is clearly stating that year is divisible by 4. If the year is divisible by 4 the remainder must be zero.

And, the expression: `year % 100 != 0` is clearly stating that year is not divisible by 100. If the year is not divisible by 100, then the remainder cannot be zero.

This pair of conditions allows years that are divisible by 4, but removes years such as 1900 which are not a leap-years.

For the second expression, I could code is as follows:

    `year % 4 == 0 and year % 4 == 0`

I could however shortcut this by writing the expression as:

    `year % 400 == 0`

by noting that any year divisible by 400 must necessarily be divisible by 4.

I must now combine these two expressions with the logical connective or, before placing it in an if statement.

The code to implement this in Python follows.

```
year = int(input("Enter the year "))

if (year % 4 == 0 and year % 100 != 0) or (year % 400 == 0) :
    leapYear = True
else :
    leapYear = False
```

To carry out (b), I need to make use of the well known mnemonic to help me remember the number of days in each month.

Thirty days have September.
April, June and November.
All the rest have thirty-one.
Excepting February alone.
And that has twenty-eight days clear.
With twenty-nine in each leap year.

We can use this rhyme, to determine the following information.

1. September (9), April (4), June (6), November (11): have 30 days.
2. January (1), March (3), May (5), July (7), August (8), October (10), December (11): have 31 days.
3. February has either 28 or 29 days. It has 29 days if the year is a leap year.

Note I am using an integer to represent each month. This makes the problem simpler.

In the first instance the expression I need to test for those months with 30 days is:

`m == 9 or m == 4 or m == 6 or m == 11`

I have used m for a variable name instead of month, because I want it all to fit on the same line.

Next, I have to check for months that have 31 days. This can be tested using the following expression:

m == 1 or m == 3 or m == 5 or m == 7 or m == 8 or m == 10 or m == 11

This will appear after `elif`.

The completed program follows.

```
year = int(input("Enter the year "))

if (year % 4 == 0 and year % 100 != 0) or (year % 400 == 0) :
    leapYear = True
else :
    leapYear = False

m = int(input("Enter month 1-12: "))

if m == 9 or m == 4 or m == 6 or m == 11 :
    days = 31
elif m == 1 or m == 3 or m == 5 or m == 7 or m == 8 or m == 10 or m == 11 :
    days = 31
else:
    if leapYear == False :
        days = 28
    else:
        days = 29

print("There are ", days , "in this month")
```

The first part of the program allows a user to input the year. The compound logical expression is now tested, to see whether it is a leap year. If it is, True is assigned to the variable leapYear. The variable leapYear, is being used as a flag that can be checked in the next part of the program.

In the last part of the program, after the user enters the month number, there is a very large if statement. The first section checks to see whether the month number corresponds to months that have 30 days. If this is false, the elif clause is used to check for months that have 31 days. Finally, if both of these fail, it must be February.

The month February can have 28 or 29 days depending on whether it is a leap year or not. This can be determined by checking the value of the flag leapYear.

Exercise 6

1. (a) Write a program that will prompt a user to enter a number between 1 and 100

   (b) Test the number input to see if it is:

   (i) even
   (ii) odd
   (iii) greater than 50

   (c) Print appropriate responses for each of these tests.

2. Write a short program which will prompt a user for an exam mark in the range 1 - 100 and will respond by printing the mark and grade.

   The rules for awarding grades are as follows:

mark	grade
79 - 100	A
67 - 78	B
54 - 66	C
40 - 54	D
< 40	F

3. A local company want to make a start at automating their payroll system. Currently the wage packets are made up individually. They get paid in cash, and have a pay receipt that details hours worked, rate of pay, overtime and gross pay etc.

   a) Assuming a basic week is 37.5 hours and any time over this is to be treated as overtime which is to be paid as 1.5 times the standard rate. Write a program that will accept input from the user for:

   Employee name, hours worked, rate of pay

   b) Continue the program by working out:

   i. the overtime worked
   ii. the basic salary (not including overtime)
   iii. the overtime pay
   iv. the gross pay (basic salary + overtime pay)

   c) Extend this calculation by including the nett pay. Nett pay is calculated by deducting 25% tax from the taxable income. Assume that the first £60 of the weekly salary is non-taxable income.

d) Print all the relevant information input, and the results of calculations in an appropriate format.

4. Write a program that will input a person's height in centimetres (cm), and weight in kilograms (kg). The output from the program will be one of the following messages: underweight, normal, or overweight, using the criteria:

   Underweight: weight < height / 2.5
   Normal: height / 2.5 ≤ weight ≤ height / 2.3
   Overweight: height / 2.3 < weight

5. Write a program that takes as input a character (a, s, m, or d), followed by two integers. The program will calculate the sum, difference, product or quotient depending on the first character input.

6. Write a program that allows a user to enter a date in the format dd/mm/yy, and outputs the date in the format **month dd, year**.

   That is my birthday will be entered as: 22/05/56

   And will be output as: May 25, 1956

   Hint: Input value as string. Use string slices to extract numeric digits. You will also have to use a very long if statement to determine the name of the month.

Lesson 7: A first look at Lists

7.1 Introduction

In many ways lists are similar to strings. You will recall:

1. A string is a sequence of characters.
2. Individual characters can be selected using the indexing operator [].
3. A string slice can be selected using the indexing operator [].
4. Strings can be joined together or concatenated with the + operator.
5. Substrings can be checked for using the in operator.
6. Strings are immutable.

The only property that is totally untrue for lists is 6. Lists are mutable. That is you can change elements of a list without having to make another copy.

A list is a sequence of values, separated by commas, and enclosed within square objects. These values can be any of any of the data types that we have seen so far and more.

You can create a list with an assignment statement. The following is valid.

```
myList = ['Tony', 2, 3.75, True]
```

I have included a list containing 4 different data types. This is permitted in Python. A session with the Python interactive shell below demonstrates these points.

```
>>> myList = ['Tony', 2, 3.75, True]
>>> myList[0]
'Tony'
>>> myList[1]
2
>>> myList[2]
3.75
>>> myList[3]
True
>>> myList[1:3]
[2, 3.75]
>>> newList = [4, 8.9]
>>> BiggerList = myList + newList
>>> BiggerList
['Tony', 2, 3.75, True, 4, 8.9]
>>> 3.75 in myList
True
>>> myList[1] = 4
>>> myList
['Tony', 4, 3.75, True]
>>>
```

You can see that the operators that we used with strings work exactly the same way when we are using them on lists.

In the first few commands, I demonstrate that the index operator [], works in the same way as for strings. That is mylist[0], and mylist[1] obtain the first and second items from the list myList etc.

The expression `myList[1:3]` obtains a sub-list or list slice containing the second and third item. That is items that have an index of 1 and 2 respectively.

The command `BiggerList = myList + newList` is an example of list concatenation. That is the lists `myList` and `newList` are joined together to form a larger list called `BiggerList`. This is analogous to string concatenation.

The in operator can be used to determine whether an item is a member of the list. So, expression `3.75 in myLists` will test whether `3.75` is in the list `myList`. If it is, this expression will evaluate to True, False otherwise.

The only difference between strings and lists are: (1) Lists are a sequence of objects, rather than characters, and (2) lists are immutable. I demonstrated the second point with the assignment statement `myList[1] = 4`. This statement changes the second element in the list from 2 to 4.

7.2 Creating and using lists of numbers

The easiest way to create a list of numbers is with an assignment statement as follows:

`numList1 = [1, 2, 3, 4, 5, 6, 7, 8, 9, 10]`

`numList2 = [11, 12, 13, 14, 15, 15, 17, 18, 19, 20]`

Note, I use square brackets to enclose the list, and each item is separated by a comma.

I can then create a larger list by combining the two lists using the + or concatenation operator.

`numList3 = numList1 + numList2`

An alternative method is to start with an empty list, and add one item at a time using the `append()` method.

An empty list is designated by a pair of square brackets with nothing enclosed.

`emptyList = []`

This is analogous to the empty string that can be created by the assignment:

`emptyString = ""`

Here an empty string is represent by a pair of quotes with nothing between them. You are free to use either single or double quotes.

I can add a number to the empty list as follows:

`emptyList.append(1)`

This adds the number 1 to the list. Subsequent use of the `append()` method will add the item to the end of the list.

A more usual method of using `append()` to add numbers to a list, is to combine this with keyboard input. The following program snippet is an example.

```
emptyList = []
number = int(input('Enter a whole number : '))
emptyList.append(number)
```

I start by creating an empty list. I then obtain an integer as input from the keyboard. This number obtained is added to the end of the list. Here, instead of using a numeric value, I have used a variable as a parameter to the `append()` method.

Once I have created my lists, there are a number of built-in list functions I can use on these lists. I will start with an interactive session in Python.

```
>>> marks = [45, 63, 72, 59]
>>> n = len(marks)
>>> n
4
>>> min(marks)
45
>>> max(marks)
72
>>> sum(marks)
239
>>> average = sum(marks) / n
>>> average
59.75
>>>
```

Here you can see that I have a list called marks that has 4 integers. This is followed by use of the `len()` function. It tells me how many items there are in the list. This is analogous to the use of `len()` to determine how many characters in a string.

There follows the use of 3 list functions, that do what you would expect them to. That is `min()` determines the smallest item, `max()` determines the largest item, and `sum()` determines the sum of all the items within the list.

Besides these, there are a number of other methods that work on lists generally, no matter what type of data is contained within a list. We have seen one of these already whilst creating a list – `append()`.

I can insert an item within a list using the `insert()` method. It has the format:

`insert(index, item)`

Here index, is used to refer to the position where you want the item inserted. Item refers to the item you want to insert.

I can remove an item from the end of a list using the `pop()` method.

I can remove the first occurrence of a specified item from a list using the `remove()` method.

Finally, I have methods that are used to change the order of items within a list.

The `reverse()` method is used to reverse the order of items, and `sort()` is used to sort the list into ascending order.

The following interactive session is used to demonstrate these methods. Note, all of the methods need the list `numList` to call them.

```
>>> numList = [10, 30, 70, 40, 20, 10, 50, 90]
>>> numList.insert(1, 20)
>>> numList
[10, 20, 30, 70, 40, 20, 10, 50, 90]
>>> a = numList.pop()
>>> numList
[10, 20, 30, 70, 40, 20, 10, 50]
>>> a
90
>>> numList.remove(20)
>>> numList
[10, 30, 70, 40, 20, 10, 50]
>>> numList.reverse()
>>> numList
[50, 10, 20, 40, 70, 30, 10]
>>> numList.sort()
>>> numList
[10, 10, 20, 30, 40, 50, 70]
>>>
```

The first example demonstrates the number 20 being inserted into the position with an index value of 1. That is, it will become the second item in the list.

The second example demonstrates the use of `pop()`. Here I have assigned the value of `pop()` to a variable called a. In this way, you can see that the last item is removed from the list and stored in a. There is no need to do this, unless you want to use this value.

In the third example, I am removing the first item in the list that has a value of 20.

The fourth example demonstrates `reverse()`. Here the items in the list have been reversed.

The last example demonstrates `sort()`. Here the new order of items, is in ascending or increasing order of size.

Other useful methods that I will mention can be used to locate a particular item within a list, and count how many occurrences there are of a particular item.

```
>>> numList = [10, 20, 30, 40, 70, 34, 89, 45, 20, 20, 67, 20]
>>> pos = numList.index(34)
>>> pos
5
>>> howMany = numList.count(20)
>>> howMany
4
>>>
```

The method `index()` in this example is used to determine the position of the first occurrence of the number 34 in the list. The method `count()` is used to determine the number of times that the number 20 occurs in the list. Note, these methods can be used on lists that contain other types of object as well.

7.3 Other ways to create lists

If you want to create a list containing the same number, or other type of list object, you can use the multiply operator.

```
>>> a = [0] * 10
>>> a
[0, 0, 0, 0, 0, 0, 0, 0, 0, 0]
>>> b = [' '] * 5
>>> b
[' ', ' ', ' ', ' ', ' ']
>>> c = [''] * 6
>>> c
['', '', '', '', '', '']
>>>
```

In the first example, I have created a list of 10 integers, each have the same value 0. In the second and third examples I have used strings. The list b contains a list of 10 spaces. The list c contains 10 empty strings.

This technique is very useful if you want to create a list of a fixed size.

An even more useful technique is the ability to create a list that contains a sequence of numbers. The range function is used to do this.

```
>>> a = range(10)
>>> len(a)
10
>>> a[0]
0
>>> a[1]
1
>>> a[2]
2
>>> a[9]
9
>>> b = range(1, 11)
>>> len(b)
10
>>> b[0]
1
>>> b[9]
10
>>> c = range(0, 11, 2)
>>> len(c)
6
>>> c[0]
0
>>> c[1]
2
>>> c[2]
4
>>>
```

The first example contains a list called a, that contains 10 integers in the range 0 to 9. Here it is assumed that the list starts with a value 0.

In the second example, the list b starts with the number 1. Here the range of numbers is 1 to 10.

Finally, in the third example, I demonstrate that you can include a step size. In this case I increase each subsequent number by 2.

The range function, if all 3 parameters are present takes the form:

```
range(start, final_number, step_size)
```

Here `start` indicates the first number in the list. The last number in the list will always have a value of `final_number` − 1, and `step_size` indicates by how much each number increases each time.

Exercise 7

What will be the resulting output from the following code? Give reasons.

1.
```
letters = ['A', 'B', 'C', 'D', 'E', 'F']
letters[2] = 'y'
letters.remove('E')
letters.append('Z')
print(letters)
```

2.
```
numbers = [1, 2, 3, 4, 5, 6, 7, 8, 9, 10]
numbers.insert(1, 1.5)
print(numbers.pop())
numbers.remove(4)
print(numbers)
```

3.
```
letters = ['A', 'B', 'C', 'D', 'E', 'F', 'G', 'H']
grades = letters[0 : 4]
letters[7] = 'U'
print(letters, grades)
```

4.
```
a = range(20)
print(a[0], a[19])
print(a[2 : 10])
```

This is supposed to be a paper exercise. But, once you have completed this, test out the above programs in Python.

Lesson 8: Iteration

8.1 Repeating a fixed number of times

The `for` statement is used in a number of programming languages to repeat a sequence of actions a fixed number of times. The same is true of Python, but it has a rather different format.

The format of a `for` statement in Python is as follows:

```
for a in <sequence> :
    < statements>
```

Here <sequence> will typically be a string or a list. You will remember that a string is a sequence of characters, and a list is a sequence of objects.

The other thing to note, is that there is a colon at the end of a `for` statement. This colon is an indication that a block of code is to follow, and that this code must be indented.

Following the colon, on the next line we have <statements>. This can represent one or more valid Python statements. Note that it is indented as it should be.

To illustrate this, I will use some examples, starting with a string.

```
>>> message = "Hello"
>>> len(message)
5
>>> for ch in message :
        print(ch)

H
e
l
l
o
>>>
```

Here ch is being used as a **control variable** to access the string `message` a character at a time. Intially ch refers to `message[0]`, and so the letter H is printed. It then moves on to the next part of the string with is `message[1]`. This refers to the letter e. This is repeated until the end of the string is reached. You will note that the statement `print(ch)` is executed 5 times. This is the number of characters in the string.

As, you will see from the following examples, it is much more common to use a list to represent <sequence> in the for statement.

The next example uses a list of strings.

```
>>> days_of_week = ['Monday', 'Tuesday', 'Wednesday', 'Thursday', 'Friday', 'Saturday', 'Sunday']
>>> len(days_of_week)
7
>>> for day in days_of_week :
        print(day)

Monday
Tuesday
Wednesday
Thursday
Friday
Saturday
Sunday
>>>
```

Here there are 7 strings in my list. The control variable `day` is used to access each item in the list in the order they appear. This is very much like the previous example that used a `for` loop to access the string a character at a time. The only difference is that lists are much more flexible as you can store many different types of object within them.

I will now move on and start using lists of numbers. For the moment my examples will have integers, but there is nothing to stop you using floats.

```
>>> numbers = [1, 2, 3, 4, 5]
>>> total = 0
>>> for number in numbers :
        total = total + number

>>> print(total)
15
>>> sum(numbers)
15
>>>
```

In the above example, I am using a for loop to sum the numbers in the list called numbers. I am using a variable called total which has an initial value of 0. This is the sum before I have added any numbers to it. Each time I access a number in the list, I add this to the total. The for loop terminates once the end of the list has been reached. The value stored in total at this point in time will be equal to the sum of the numbers.

I remind you that we could have used the `sum()` built-in function to obtain the same result. This is much shorter and easier.

But, this function could not be used for more complicated calculations such as compute the sum of the squares of the first 5 integers. I can easily modify the previous example to do this.

```
>>> numbers = [1, 2, 3, 4, 5]
>>> total = 0
>>> for number in numbers :
        total = total + number ** 2

>>> print(total)
55
>>>
```

8.2 Use of the `range()` function in for loops

We have already seen that the `range()` function generates a list of numbers. If we were to wish to use a larger list of numbers, say numbers in the range 0 to 99, it would be easier to use `range(100)` rather than have to list each of the 100 numbers individually.

In many cases, we want to start with the number 1 and end at 100. This can be obtained with `range(1, 101)`.

Sometimes, we may want to go up in fives or some other number each time. That is we want to increment the number by 5 each time instead of 1. This can be achieved with `range(0, 101, 5)`. This will create the sequence 0, 5, 10, ……, 100.

I will start with a short program to calculate the sum of the squares of the first 100 integers.

```
>>> total = 0
>>> for x in range(1, 101) :
        total = total + x ** 2

>>> print(total)
338350
>>>
```

The `range()` function above will generate a list with 100 numbers in the range 1 to 100. This is the preferred way of doing things if you want to iterate over a large list of numbers.

In many situations, you may want to enter the numbers from a keyboard. The following program illustrates this.

```
# Sum numbers entered at the keyboard

total = 0.0
n = int(input("Enter the number of numbers : "))

# repeat n times
for x in range(n) :
    num = float(input("Enter next number : "))
    total = total + num

print("The sum of these numbers is ", total)
```

The variable n must be an integer, because the for loop needs to repeat a whole number of times. The function call `range(n)` will generate a sequence of numbers in the range 0 to n-1. The main thing is that there are n numbers in the list, and this is how many times the for loop will repeat. I have chosen to convert all input for the numbers entered to be of type float. This means that my program can accept both integers and floats without any problem.

```
Enter the number of numbers : 5
Enter next number : 3
Enter next number : 4.5
Enter next number : 6.2
Enter next number : 6
Enter next number : 2.9
The sum of these numbers is   22.599999999999998
```

As you can see from the output, you have to be careful using floating point values. If you check with a calculator, you will observe that the value should be 22.6. The reason that we did not get this result, is because floating point numbers cannot be represented exactly, so there will always be slight errors.

This problem can be sorted out by rounding the answer to 2 decimal places. We could replace the print function with the following to achieve this.

```
print("The sum of these numbers is ", round(total, 2))
```

I will now include another example program to demonstrate use of the `for` loop.

```
# Multiplication tables

n = int(input("Enter a number for times table : "))
print(n, " times table")
print("------------------")

for x in range(1, 11) :
    print(x, " times ", n, " = ", x * n)
```

Here n is used to indicate the times table to be printed. Within the for statement the function call `range(1, 11)` will generate a sequence of numbers in the range 1 to 10. The control variable x takes the value of each of the numbers in the sequence, starting with 1. This value is also used in the calculation x * n. The program produces the following output.

```
Enter a number for times table : 7
7  times table
------------------
1  times  7  =  7
2  times  7  =  14
3  times  7  =  21
4  times  7  =  28
5  times  7  =  35
6  times  7  =  42
7  times  7  =  49
8  times  7  =  56
9  times  7  =  63
10 times  7  =  70
>>>
```

8.3 While loops as an alternative to for loops

Most of what we have already done using for loops, we can do with while loops. If we were to loop a fixed number of times using a while loop, we would have to make use of a counter to tell when it is time to stop.

The general format for a while statement in Python is:

```
while <condition> :
    <statements>
```

Here <condition> can be replaced by any Boolean expression, and <statements> can be replaced with a block of one or more statements that you want to execute.

I will start by demonstrating how you can use a while statement to loop a fixed number of times.

```
count = 0                  # initialize a counter to 0
while count < 6 :
    print("Hello")
    count = count + 1      # Increment counter each time
```

In this program, a variable called count is used to count how many times the actions are to be repeated. It needs to be initialized to 0. Within the header of the while loop, there is a condition that is evaluated each time. While this condition is true, the statements that follow are executed. As soon as it becomes false, the loop terminates. This loop terminates when count has a value of 6.

Within the body of the while loop, there are two statements that can be executed. The first prints Hello to the screen. The second adds one to the variable called count.

I can also use this technique to redo the program for multiplication tables, but to use a while loop instead.

```
n = int(input("Enter a number for times table : "))
print(n, " times table")
print("------------------")

x = 1
while x < 11 :
    print(x, " times ", n, " = ", x * n)
    x = x + 1
```

The first part of the program has been copied from the previous program for multiplication tables. Here I am using x as a control variable to count how many times the actions are repeated. The variable x is also used within the print statement and is used to calculate the product x * n.

8.4 Using a while loop to terminate input.

Suppose I want to perform some sort of calculation using numbers that have been entered at the keyboard. If I don't know how many numbers I am going to enter in advance, I cannot do as I have previously done and enter the numbers. I need a way to indicate that I wish to terminate the loop.

A way round this problem is to introduce a data value that cannot be part of the data. This value is often called a rogue value. So, for instance, if I have to enter a sequence of positive numbers, I can indicate that I have finished by entering a negative number.

The following program computes the average from a sequence of numbers entered at the keyboard.

```
n = 0
count = 0
sum = 0
while n != -1 :      # Terminate loop if n = -1
    n = int(input("Enter next positive number (-1 to terminate) : "))
    if n >= 0 :      # Number must be positive
        count += 1
        sum += n
average = sum / count
print("Average = ", average)
```

At the beginning of the program, I have initialized a number of variables. I need to set n equal to a value, because I need to carry out the test n != 0. The variable count is used to determine how many numbers are to be summed. The variable sum is used to obtain the total sum of all the positive numbers input.

Within the body of the loop, the `if` statement tests whether the number is positive. If it is, I know this is a valid number and can be added to the sum.

The statement `count += 1` is an abbreviated form of `count = count + 1`. It is used to count how many numbers have been added.

Likewise, the statement `sum += n` is an abbreviated form of `sum = sum + n`. The variable sum has an initial value of 0. Then, each time a positive number is entered at the keyboard, that number is added to the current total stored in sum. When the while loop terminates, the value of the variable sum is equal to the total sum of the positive numbers input.

8.5 Terminating a while loop when a certain value has been reached

This section demonstrates a more normal use of the while loop that you cannot easily do using a for loop. I will start with a problem.

Problem specification

Sam is saving for a deposit for a flat. He is confident that he can save £300 each month to put towards the deposit. To make the money go further, he intends to put the money into a savings account that pays interest. The interest rate offered is currently 3.75% per annum, and is paid monthly. He needs to save £30000. How long will he take to save this amount in months?

Analysis of problem

The monthly interest will be 3.75 % ÷ 12. It is best to express this as a decimal. That is: $monthly\ interest = \frac{3.75}{100 \times 12}$.

At the end of each month, you will be adding £300 to the sum and the interest on the sum.

To work out the new total from the previous sum, it is easier to work out the new amount by multiplying the previous sum by (1 + R), where R is the monthly interest expressed as a decimal.

The loop will stop when the sum exceeds 30000.

Program

```
#    Time taken in months to save a deposit of £30000

yR = 3.75 / 100      #    yearly interest rate
mR = yR / 12         #    monthly interest rate
months = 0
total = 0.0

while total < 30000 :
    total += 300
    total *= (1 + mR)
    months += 1

print('Sam has saved ', round(total, 2))
print('It took him ', months, ' months to save this amount')
```

The main thing I want to discuss about this program is the while loop. The test condition is `total < 30000`. While this is true we need to keep going. Each time the loop is repeated, 300 is added to the total. This value is then multiplied by (1+ mR) to give the new amount that includes interest. There is a variable called `months`. This is used as a counter. It counts how many months are needed. At the beginning of the while loop, the total is compared each time with 30000. If total ≥ 30000, the while loop terminates.

When the loop terminates, the two print statements that follow are executed. These print out the total saved and how many months are required to save this amount.

```
Sam has saved  30032.76
It took him  87  months to save this amount
>>>
```

8.6 Using break to terminate a loop

The break statement can be used to terminate a loop. I will look at this, by solving a problem in two different ways.

Problem

The equation $x^2 + x = 11$ has a solution which is slightly larger than 2. Find the solution to 2 decimal places by calculating $x^2 + x$ for values of x that has an initial value of 2 and increases in steps of 0.01. The program loop will stop when $x^2 + x \geq 11$.

```
#    Numerical solution - method 1

x = 2.0
y = x ** 2 + x
while y < 11 :
    x += 0.01
    y = x ** 2 + x

print("x = \t", round(x, 2), "\ty = \t", y)
```

This is the same, method used previously.

The next program will use a break statement to achieve the same result.

```
#    Numerical solution - method 2

x = 2.0
while True :
    y = x ** 2 + x
    if y >= 11 :
        break
    else:
        x += 0.01

print("x = \t", round(x, 2), "\ty = \t", y)
```

With this version of the program, the condition tested for the while loop is always true. Without the break statement, this would be an infinite loop. That is, it would never stop. There is an if statement within the while loop that tests for y ≥ 11. If this is true, the break statement is executed. This statement causes control of the program to resume after the while loop.

With either program, I obtain the output below.

```
x =     2.86   y =      11.039599999999878
>>>
```

8.7 Nested loops

Earlier, there was a program that produced a multiplication table. This time I want to create a table that includes all ten times tables. I will achieve this by using a nested for loop. A nested loop is just a loop inside a loop.

```
# Multiplication tables using a nested loop

for x in range(1, 11) :
    for y in range(1, 11) :
        print(x * y, "\t", end = "")
```

When you have a nested loop like this, it is important to remember that most of the action takes place within the inner loop. After x is set to 1, control passes to the inner loop. Here y is set to 1, and then the print statement is executed. After this, y is set to 2 and x * y is calculated before being printed out. This continues until y has taken all the values from 1 to 10.

In a sense, the variable x determines the values in each row, and the y variable determines the value in each column going across each row.

Another thing I need to mention, is the inclusion of end = "" at the end of the print statement. This prevents you going onto the next line until an iteration of the inner for loop has completed.

The output is as follows.

```
1    2    3    4    5    6    7    8    9    10
2    4    6    8    10   12   14   16   18   20
3    6    9    12   15   18   21   24   27   30
4    8    12   16   20   24   28   32   36   40
5    10   15   20   25   30   35   40   45   50
6    12   18   24   30   36   42   48   54   60
7    14   21   28   35   42   49   56   63   70
8    16   24   32   40   48   56   64   72   80
9    18   27   36   45   54   63   72   81   90
10   20   30   40   50   60   70   80   90   100
```

Exercise 8

1. Write a program that allows a user to enter their name. The program will then print out their name 5 times.

2. Write a program to convert a temperature measured in degrees Centigrade to degrees Fahrenheit. Modify this program so that the temperature in Centigrade is worked out for temperatures in the range 0 - 100C and so that the temperature in degrees Centigrade goes up in increments of 5 degrees. You output should be a neat table showing temperature in degrees C, and the corresponding temperature in degrees F.

3. Write a program to compute factorials given that :

    5 factorial (5!) = 5 × 4 × 3 × 2 × 1

4. Write a program that will test for prime numbers.

    (a) A prime number has two divisors only (1 and itself). Start by dividing by 2, then increase by 1 each time until you reach a value which is one less than the number itself.

    (b) You may want to use the % operator to test for a remainder on division. If the number is divisible, there should be no remainder.

    (c) Test your program with numbers that you know are prime – 2, 3, 5, 7 etc.

5. Write a program that will add first 100 natural numbers. That is, sum all of the terms in the series 1 + 2 + 3 + 4 + ... + 99 +100. You are to include a loop to achieve this.

    There is a formula that can be used to calculate the sum to n terms given by:

    $$S_n = \frac{n(n+1)}{2}$$

    Here, S_n is to be interpreted as the sum of n terms in this series. Use the value n = 100 in your program to check that you obtain the same result as in the first part of the program

6. If you really want a challenge, check out Project Euler online. You can go directly to the archived problems by using the following link.

    ```
    https://projecteuler.net/archives
    ```

    Start with problem 1. I feel that this should be accessible.

Lesson 9: Functions

9.1 A first look at functions in Python

As programs get larger, it is important to be able to split the program into smaller components. Most programming languages achieve this by providing constructs such as **functions** or **procedures** that break the program up into a number of self-contained modules that communicate with each other. Each of these modules should be able to perform a useful task and should be available for use anywhere in the program. Such a facility makes a program easier to develop, easier to debug and improves the readability of the program.

In very simple terms:

1. A **function** is a block of code containing statements that perform a calculation and returns an answer called the **return value**.

2. A **procedure** is a block of code containing statements, that when executed perform some actions that satisfy a certain task. In practical terms, this usually means working something out and then printing out the answer.

3. The Python language only has functions. The equivalent of a procedure in Python is a function that does not have a return value.

You have probably met functions already in the mathematics classroom. In mathematics, a function is a mapping that connects two sets of numbers. One set is called the domain. These can be thought of as possible input values or arguments. There is also a rule that, for any given input value, will produce a single output value. This set of possible output values is in mathematics referred to as the range.

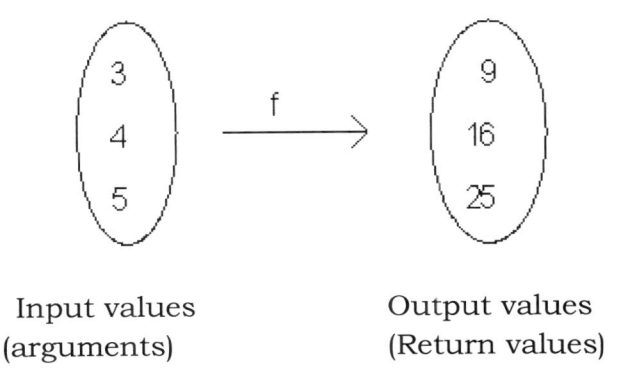

Input values (arguments)   Output values (Return values)

The above function f computes the square number of its input value.

Using standard mathematical notation, we could state:

f(3) = 9, f(4) = 16, f(5) = 25

We could of course create our own function in Python to do this.

```
def f(x) :
    square = x ** 2
    return square

num = int(input("Enter a whole number : "))

sq = f(num)      #   This is a function call
print("The square of ", num, " is ", sq)
```

Typical output would look like this.

```
Enter a whole number : 7
The square of  7 is  49
>>>
```

The first part of the program contains a **function definition**. A function definition always starts with the keyword def. This is followed by the name of the function, and its parameters. The **parameters** are the variables within the brackets. These correspond to the possible input values within the domain. At the end of the **function header**, there is a colon. The colon is there to indicate that what follows is a block of code and so must be indented.

This block of code is called the **function body**. In this instance, within the function body there is a simple calculation, and a **return statement**. The return statement is used to pass a value to the calling function.

Further down in the program you will see a function call: `sq = f(num)`. When this statement is executed, the value of the variable num is passed to the function `f()` that has been called. In the example run shown, num has a value of 7. This value is assigned to the parameter of the function called x. So, now x = 7. This particular parameter passing mechanism is called "**call-by-value**".

Within the function body, the value of x is used to calculate a square number which is assigned to the variable called square. It is the value of this variable that appears in the return statement. Execution of the return statement passes the value of square to the calling statement. Here the return value is assigned to the variable sq.

This is the normal way to call functions. An alternative would be to print the result directly. We could, if we wanted insert the function call within a print statement as follows.

```
print("The square of ", num, " is ", f(num))
```

9.2 More examples of functions that return a value.

In this section, I intend to show a variety of example. Not all of these will return a number. The examples below return a string.

```
#   Obtain name of a day in the week - version 1

def getDay(n) :
    if n == 1 :
        return "Monday"
    elif n == 2 :
        return "Tuesday"
    elif n == 3 :
        return "Wednesday"
    elif n == 4 :
        return "Thursday"
    elif n == 5 :
        return "Friday"
    elif n == 6 :
        return "Saturday"
    elif n == 7 :
        return "Sunday"
    else :
        return "Invalid day number"

dayNumber = int(input("Enter day number 1 to 7 : "))
day = getDay(dayNumber)
print("you wanted ", day)
```

In this example, the value of the day number is used to determine the corresponding name of a day. A large `if` statement is used with many `elif` clauses for this purpose. This is the correct thing to do, because the tests are mutually exclusive. For this reason, you don't have to worry that there are many return statements within this function. Only one of them can be executed for each function call.

A shorter version that uses lists, is shown below.

```
#   Obtain name of a day in the week - version 2

def getDay(n) :
    days1 = ['Monday', 'Tuesday', 'Wednesday' 'Thursday']
    days2 = ['Friday', 'Saturday', 'Sunday']
    days = days1 + days2
    return days[n-1]

dayNumber = int(input("Enter day number 1 to 7 : "))
day = getDay(dayNumber)
print("you wanted ", day)
```

Functions can be used to check the status of something. In this case the return value is of type Boolean. The following example function is used to check whether a letter is a vowel.

```
def isVowel(ch) :
    vowels = ['A', 'E', 'I', 'O', 'U', 'a', 'e', 'i', 'o', 'u']
    if ch in vowels :
        return True
    else :
        return False

letter = input("Enter a letter ")
if isVowel(letter) :
    print("Letter is a vowel")
else :
    print("Letter is a consonant")
```

A sample output follows.

```
Enter a letter A
Letter is a vowel
>>>
```

In this example, a list is used to store possible vowels. So, if the character is a vowel, it must be in the list called vowels. If it is, True is returned, otherwise False.

I have inserted my function call into an `if` statement. This is a normal thing to do as the return value is of type Boolean. In the sample run, I have entered the letter 'A', and so I would expect a return value of True.

This means that `isVowel(letter)` has a value of True, so my if statement is equivalent to `if True`, so on this occasion, I would expect to get the message "Letter is a vowel".

Note: `if isVowel(letter)` is commonly written as: `if isVowel(letter) == True`. This is not necessary. The first example is obvious, and in many ways clearer.

9.3 Functions with no return statement.

In many other programming languages, procedures are available as well as functions. A function that has no return statement is equivalent to a procedure. These functions are typically used to produce either input or output. They can also be used to perform calculations and then print out the results rather than return a single value that can either be printed out or stored in a variable.

As a first example, I will start with a function that just prints a message. These are useful to provide instructions. The following example displays the menu options.

```
def printMessage() :
    print("\tMenu options")
    print("1.\t Watch TV")
    print("2.\t Go for a walk")
    print("3.\t Do your homework")
    print("4.\t Have your dinner")

printMessage()
```

program output

```
        Menu options
1.      Watch TV
2.      Go for a walk
3.      Do your homework
4.      Have your dinner
>>>
```

All this function does is print out 4 strings. It is likely to be used just before you have to input your choice. Notice, there are no parameters for this function, and no return statement.

Note also, that the function call is not assigned to a variable. This is because there is no useful return value that can be assigned to a variable.

I will now include a function that does some calculations, and then prints out the results. So, this too is also a procedure, as there is no return statement

```
import math

def circleFacts(r) :
    circ = 2 * math.pi * r
    area = math.pi * r ** 2
    print("Radius of circle is : ", r)
    print("Circumference is : ", round(circ, 3))
    print("Area is : ", round(area, 3))

radius = float(input("Enter a radius : "))
circleFacts(radius)
```

This function has a single **formal parameter** called r. This takes the value of the radius – the **actual parameter**. The function calculates the circumference and area of the circle, and then prints out the relevant results.

It is common to use a mixture of functions and procedures in your program. The following has a number of functions to obtain customer details, and a procedure to output some results.

This program has a number of function definitions that form the bulk of the program.

```python
def getName() :
    custName = input("Enter customer name : ")
    return custName

def getRateOfPay() :
    hourlyRate = float(input("Enter hourly rate of pay : "))
    return hourlyRate

def getHoursWorked() :
    hoursWorked = int(input("Enter a whole number for hours worked : "))
    return hoursWorked

def displayCustDetails(name, rate, hours) :
    print("Customer Name : ", name)
    print("Hourly rate of pay : ", rate)
    print("Number of hours worked : ", hours)
    nettPay = hours * rate
    print("Nett pay : ", nettPay)

def custPay():
    cName = getName()
    hRate = getRateOfPay()
    hWorked = getHoursWorked()
    displayCustDetails(cName, hRate, hWorked)

custPay()
```

```
Enter customer name : Tony Hawken
Enter hourly rate of pay : 32.50
Enter a whole number for hours worked : 24
Customer Name :  Tony Hawken
Hourly rate of pay :  32.5
Number of hours worked :  24
Nett pay :  780.0
```

The first 3 functions are used to obtain input from the keyboard. You need to have a return value to obtain this input.

The fourth function is used to display the results.

The fifth function calls all of the other functions. The body of this function is made up of 4 function calls. This just goes to show that you can call functions from within another function.

So, to run all of these functions, I just need to run the function call `custPay()`.

9.4 Local variables and scope

As your programs get larger, you may have problems with variables with the same name. Which variable you are able to access depends on its **scope**.

In Python, unless you state otherwise, all variables are **local**. That means that they can only be accessed in the immediate part of the program where they are defined. So if a variable is defined inside the body of a function, we say that that **variable is local** to that function. We can also say that the **scope of the variable** is the function where it is defined.

To demonstrate this, I have included a silly program.

```
def fun() :
    a = 3         # The variable a is local to this function
    print(a)

fun()             # Here I have access to variable a within function fun()

a = 5
print(a)
```

Within the function called `fun()`, I have a variable called a. It can only be accessed whilst inside this function. So, the print statement inside the function is able to access it. The only legitimate way of passing this value outside the function is to use a return statement.

The variable a defined outside the function is a different variable, and also has a different value. The scope of this variable is the calling part of the program.

Some people will try and get round these rules of scope by using **global variables**. A global variable can be used anywhere in the program. But there is a reason to encourage using local variables. Local variables are used precisely so they cannot be accessed anywhere else except within the scope where they are defined. This is to protect the data. It stops people accidentally updating a variable without realising it. Generally speaking, global variables should not be used at all.

9.5 Palindromes

This example program includes a function to determine whether a word is a palindrome or not.

A palindrome is a word which, if it is read backwards, will give you the same word. Examples of palindromes are radar, eve, level, civic, noon, rotator. You could also include numeric examples such as 909, 12321 etc.

Observations

It is normal to store words as a string. We could then compare individual characters to see if they are the same. In particular, we may start comparing the first letter with the last, the second letter with the second from last etc.

Let's look at a palindrome.

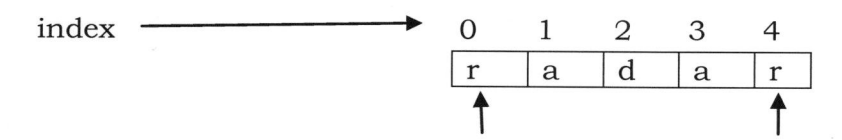

```
index            0   1   2   3   4
                 r   a   d   a   r
```

Initially we need to compare the first letter with the last. That is `word[0] == word[4]`. We also have `word[1] == word[3]`. We can make use of the fact that the length of the string is determined by `len(word)`.

```
>>> word = "radar"
>>> n = len(word)
>>> for i in range(n) :
        print(i, n - 1 - i, word[i] == word[n - 1 - i])

0 4 True
1 3 True
2 2 True
3 1 True
4 0 True
>>>
```

This appears to be the basis for a very simple algorithm to determine whether a word is a palindrome.

The algorithm could be expressed as follows:

for each letter in the word given by word[i]
    if word[i] != word[n – 1 – i]   # if any of these letters are different,
        return false   # word is not a palindrome

return true   # If I reach this statement, must be a palindrome

In Python, this algorithm becomes:

```
def isPalindrome(x) :
    x2 = str(x)
    n = len(x2)
    palindrome = True
    for i in range(n) :
        if x2[i] != x2[n - 1 - i] :
            palindrome = False
    return palindrome

# Test out isPalindrome with a number of words

word = "something"
while word != "" :
    word = input("Enter a word, quit by just pressing return : ")
    if word != "" :
        if isPalindrome(word) :
            print(word, " is a a palindrome")
        else :
            print(word, " is not a palindrome")
```

A sample output follows.

```
Enter a word, quit by just pressing return : radar
radar  is a a palindrome
Enter a word, quit by just pressing return : noot
noot  is not a palindrome
Enter a word, quit by just pressing return : noon
noon  is a a palindrome
Enter a word, quit by just pressing return : rotator
rotator  is a a palindrome
Enter a word, quit by just pressing return : 909
909  is a a palindrome
Enter a word, quit by just pressing return :
>>>
```

In the while loop, there is a nested if statement. So, it would appear that I have gone against my own advice by using it. Had I used the test,

```
if  word != "" and isPalindrome(word)
```

when I terminated the loop, by just pressing return, I would get the message "is not a palindrome", even though no word had been entered.

9.6 Recursive functions

Recursion is the technique of describing something in terms of itself. So a recursive procedure or function is said to be self-referential. A function that calls itself is called a recursive function. Recursion is an alternative method to iterative algorithms.

The simplest example that appears in many books dealing with the topic of recursion is factorials. One way of describing a factorial is to give an example like the following and then generalise it.

$$5! = 5 \times 4 \times 3 \times 2 \times 1 \qquad \text{(where ! is a short-hand for factorial)}$$

More generally we could say :

$$n! = n \times (n-1) \times (n-2) \times \ldots \times 3 \times 2 \times 1$$

To be more accurate we would also have to state that $0! = 1$.

We could implement this non-recursively using the following function. Here a for loop is used to make sure that we multiply the necessary numbers together.

```
def factorial(n):
    product = 1
    for c in range(1, n+1):
        product *= c
    return product

num = 6
result = factorial(num)
print(result)
```

But, if you look at the first definition again, you will notice that it can easily be expanded as follows:

$$n! = n \times (n-1) \times (n-2) \times \ldots \times 3 \times 2 \times 1$$

$$n! = n \times (n-1)!$$
$$(n-1)! = (n-1) \times (n-2)!$$
$$(n-2)! = (n-2) \times (n-3)!$$
.
.
$$3! = 3 \times 2!$$
$$2! = 2 \times 1!$$
$$1! = 1 \times 0! \qquad \text{And, we know that } 0! = 1 \text{ by definition.}$$

These expressions are called recurrence relations.

If we take the most general expression which is:

```
n! = n × (n-1)!
```

and the terminating condition 0! = 1, we can easily write a recursive function to do the same thing.

```
def factorial(n) :
    if n == 1 :
        return 1
    else :
        return n * factorial(n-1)

num = 6
result = factorial(num)
print(result)
```

Here, one of the first things you need to think about is what is the terminating condition. In this case, it is when n = 1. The else part of the if statement carries out a recursive function call.

Now is the time to explain how recursion works. The following demonstrates the recursive evaluation of 5 factorial.

		Stack	Stack	Pop items off stack
	0!	1	1	
	1!	1 × 0!	1× 1	1
	2!	2 × 1!	2 × 1	2
	3!	3 × 2!	3 × 2	6
	4!	4 × 3!	4 × 6	24
Push items on stack	5!	5 × 4!	5 × 24	120

Each time a recursive call is made, it is stored on the system stack ready to be used at a later time. When a termination condition arises (0! = 1), this stops. The first item is popped off the stack and the value substituted into the expression below. This continues until the last item on the stack is removed. By this time 5! has been evaluated.

Exercise 9

1. Write a function to compute the cube of a number. The header for the function definition should be:

   ```
   def cube(n) :
   ```

   Include one or more function calls to test your function `cube()`.

2. Write a function to compute the hypotenuse of a right-angled triangle given the other two sides. Include one or more function calls that print the length of the 3 sides of the triangle.

3. Write a program, to perform a temperature conversion for values 0^0C to 100^0C in increments of . The program should have a function to perform the conversion, and will print out both temperatures (Centigrade and Fahrenheit) in a neat table to 2 decimal places.

4. Write a function definition called `sumSquares()`. The function will return an integer which is the sum of the squares of the integers 1 to n. Write a program that uses this function to print out the sum of the first 20 squares, and the sum of the first 100 squares.

5. Write a function to display a menu such as:

   ```
                MENU
                -------
       1.       Play Space Invaders
       2.       Play PACMAN
       3.       Play Super Mario
       4.       Quit Menu
   ```

   (a) Test the function by including in your program a function call

   (b) Modify your main program so that a user is prompted to enter a number corresponding to the desired choice.

   (c) Include this in a while loop which terminates when they choose the option to quit the menu.

6. Fibonacci numbers can be computed by adding together the two previous numbers. The following is a Fibonacci series:

   1, 1, 2, 3, 5, 8, 13, 21, 34, 55, 89 .... etc.

   Write a function call fib that will compute the nth Fibonacci number given the following rules:

   fib(1) = 1, fib(2) = 1, fib(n+2) = fib(n) + fib(n+1)

Lesson 10: Using lists as arrays

10.1 Introduction

When processing large amounts of similar data, it makes sense if we can treat this data as a whole. Then we can easily repeat the same operation on the data. In most languages you have a data structure called an **array**.

Python has lists that can be used as if they are arrays. You have to remember that there are many things that you can do with lists that are available in Python that you cannot do with more traditional arrays. For this reason we will restrict ourselves to the type of operations that are available in more traditional array processing.

A collection of like data items is called an array. In more traditional programming languages, these are of fixed length and must contain the same type of data. They usually have to be declared in advance and be of a fixed predetermined size. Declaring such an array allocates storage in memory big enough to hold that fixed number of data items. Below are examples in C++ demonstrating how arrays are declared before they can be used.

```
int numbers[10];     // Array to store 10 integers
char name[20];       // Array to store 20 characters
```

Note in C++, and many other languages, once the arrays have been created, you cannot change their size. You can only change the data items within the array.

In Python, there is no need to have the same type of data in a list. Nor do we have to declare it beforehand. The size of a list can be changed. It can shrink or it can expand. But, in this section, I will be writing code, which mimics more traditional languages such as C++.

In Python, if we must have a fixed length list to store floats, we could do the following.

```
numbers = [0] * 10      # Fixed length list with 10 integers
```

Note to do this, we have had to store a value of 0 for each element in the list. You can think of these as default values that can be overwritten.

Individual elements of an array are accessed by reference to an **index**. An index is merely a number that refers to the position within an array. In C++ the first element has the index 0. The same is true of lists in Python. As you have seen previously, both strings and lists are indexed, and the first index value is 0. Below is an illustration of an array of floats. It does not matter whether it was created in C++ or Python.

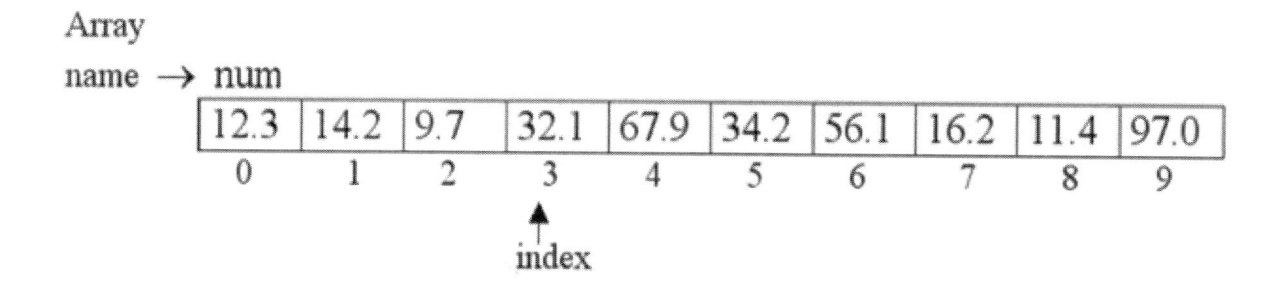

Array
name → num

| 12.3 | 14.2 | 9.7 | 32.1 | 67.9 | 34.2 | 56.1 | 16.2 | 11.4 | 97.0 |
| 0 | 1 | 2 | 3 | 4 | 5 | 6 | 7 | 8 | 9 |

↑
index

To create the previous list in Python, we could use the following code.

```
num = [12.3, 14.2, 9.7, 32.1, 67.9, 34.2, 56.1, 16.2, 11.4, 97.0]
```

You have the facility to create arrays in this manner using C++ as well. In C++ you can do the same thing by writing the following.

```
float num[] = {12.3, 14.2, 9.7, 32.1, 67.9, 34.2, 56.1, 16.2, 11.4,97.0};
```

If I want to display the first two elements in num, in Python, I could write:

```
print(num[0])
print(num[1])
```

But the more normal way to create an array of 10 floats using C++ would be:

```
float num[10];
```

This creates and array called num and allocates storage big enough for 10 floats. Typically a float is 4 bytes of storage, so 40 bytes will be allocated. Like Python, the name num is a reference to the array. It points to the storage in memory which contains the array.

If we wanted to mimic this in Python, we could do the following:

```
num = [0] * 10
```

In this case, the array will be populated with a value of 0 each time.

Because we can refer to each element in turn using its index, it is very easy to use a for loop to process the data in an array, making use of the control variable within the for loop to identify the item of data to be processed.

So, if we wanted to create a list with the numbers 1 to 10 in it, we could update num using the following code:

```
for i in range(len(num)) :
    num[i] = i + 1
```

Here `len(num)` will have a value of 10. The function call `range(10)` is equivalent to the list [0, 1, 2, 3, 4, 5, 6, 7, 8, 9]. So, the index i in the for loop will take the values 0 to 9. Each time, I am storing the value of i + 1 into the list. This will overwrite the value 0 that was present beforehand.

I can also use a for loop to display the contents of num:

```
for i in range(len(num)) :
    print(num[i], "\t", end = "")
```

And, if I run all the code related to num, I obtain the following.

1	2	3	4	5	6	7	8	9	10

Note, in Python, I could have also written `print(num)`, without needing the for loop. But we are going to have to place a restriction on what we will do here, as you cannot display the contents of an array in C++, other than by displaying each item one by one.

10.2   An example of array processing

In this section, I will be looking at how to reproduce typical array processing, as seen in a language such as C++. I will include a single example which illustrates the typical operations.

```
# 1.    Create an array of 10 floats
a = [0.0] * 10

# 2.    Input 10 floats and store in array
for x in range(10) :
    a[x] = float(input("Enter next number : "))

# 3.    Display contents of array
for x in range(10) :
    print(a[x], "\t", end = "")

# 4.    Sum elements of array
sum = 0
for x in range(10) :
    sum += a[x]

# 5.    Display smallest element
min = a[0]
for x in range(1, 10) :
    if a[x] < min :
        min = a[x]
print("Smallest number is ", min)
```

I have numbered each section of code in the comments to make this easier to discuss.

1. A fixed length array can be created using the multiply operator. Each element in this array has a value of 0.0.

2. I use an input statement within a for loop to enter 10 numbers that overwrite the previous values stored in the array.

3. The contents of the array are printed one at a time by including a print statement within a for loop. Note if I were to program using a Python style, I would have just included the statement `print(a)`, which would have just printed the list in one go.

4. To sum the elements, I initialize a variable called sum to 0. Then, within a for loop, I add to sum the value of each element. If I were to do this the Python way, I would just write `print(sum(a))` in place of this block of code.

5. Finally, to obtain the minimum value of all the elements of the array, I start by assigning the value of `a[0]` to min. I then test each of the remaining elements against the value of min. If an element `a[x] < min`, I assign the value of `a[x]` to min. If I were to ignore the constraints I have imposed, I could have just used the `min()` function available in Python. I could have then replaced all of this code with `print("The smallest element is ", min(a))`. Likewise, if I needed the maximum, I could have used the function `max()`.

10.3 Using functions to process arrays

In this worked example, I want to show how arrays can be processed using functions. For this example, I will be using two datasets that represent the heights of people in two classes. They are represented by the following data sets.

```
#   Define data sets
heights = [1.68, 1.84, 1.47, 1.57, 1.64, 1.77, 1.53, 1.64, 1.81, 1.89]
heights2 = [1.58, 1.94, 1.55, 1.75, 1.69, 1.47, 1.48, 1.34, 1.72]
```

I want to obtain various measures of average. In the first instance I will be looking at the mean. In mathematics you will know that the mean is given by:

$mean = \frac{\Sigma x}{n}$. This is interpreted as the sum of the data divided by the number of items.

I can pass the name of the array as a parameter of the function that will calculate the mean. I then need to be able to sum all of the numbers in the array, and then divide by the number of numbers. I will use the same method I used previously to sum the numbers. The mean function follows.

```
def mean(a) :
    sum = 0.0
    for c in range(len(a)) :
        sum += a[c]
    average = sum / len(a)
    return average
```

This function takes the name of the function. Here the formal parameter is a. It then uses a for loop to add up the numbers in the array. The average is determined by dividing this sum by the length of the array. The length of the array is the number of numbers in the array.

To use this function I need a function call. The following function calls will compute the mean for arrays heights and heights2.

```
print("Mean of heights = ", round(mean(heights), 2))
print("Mean of heights2 = ", round(mean(heights2), 2))
```

For the first function call, the actual parameter is heights. The formal parameter for the function mean() is a. So, when I look inside the function body, any reference to the name a is really referring to the array heights. After average has been calculated within the body of the function, this value is returned. It is this value that is printed out in the print statement.

I now propose we consider working out another type of average – the median. The median value of a data set is the middle value, once you have sorted the data. So, to work out the median, I could use the sort() method.

There is another problem when you want to work out the median of a set of numbers. If you have an even number of numbers, the middle value is not present in the data set. To illustrate what I mean, I will list a sorted version of array heights.

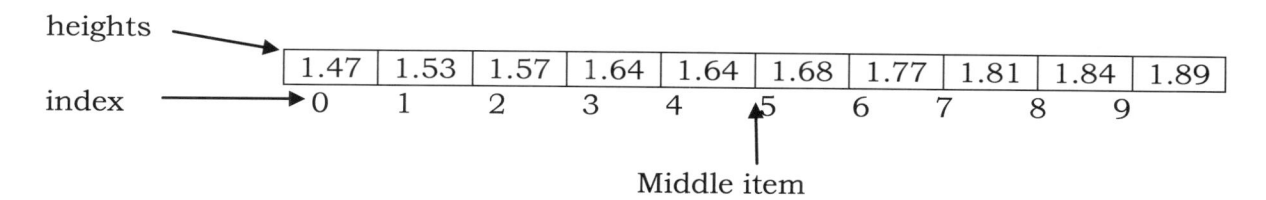

heights

1.47	1.53	1.57	1.64	1.64	1.68	1.77	1.81	1.84	1.89

index → 0   1   2   3   4   5   6   7   8   9

Middle item

From the diagram above, you can see that the middle item is between the fifth and sixth item. That is we need to obtain the average of a[4] and a[5].

In school, in your mathematics class you may have been given a rule to work out the median. If there are n items, then $middle\ item = \frac{n+1}{2}$. In the case of heights, this will give us a value of 5.5. This indicates that we want the average of the fifth and sixth values.

The array heights2 has 9 items, and this is an odd number. In this case, the middle item will be the fifth item. We can use the same rule, namely $middle\ item = \frac{n+1}{2}$. In this case, given that n = 9, we obtain a value of 5. That is the median is the fifth data item.

The completed function is below.

```
def median(a) :
    if len(a) % 2 == 0 :               # Even number of items
        m = len(a) // 2
        value = (a[m - 1] + a[m]) / 2
    else :                             # odd number of items
        m = (len(a) -1) // 2
        value = a[m]
    return value
```

Within the body of the `median()` function, there is an if statement that tests whether the number of items in the array is even. Using our formula $middle\ item = \frac{n+1}{2}$ this tells us, if I let m = n//2, then the median will be the average of (m-1)th and (m)th terms. Remember, indexes of an array start with 0, so I need to work out:

```
(a[m - 1] + a[m]) / 2
```

Calculating the median for an odd number of numbers is somewhat easier. I am sure you can work this out, and then compare it with the code in the `median()` function.

To try this out, I need some function calls. Below, I have included sufficient code to try this out

```
heights.sort()
print("heights = ", heights)
print("Median value of heights = ", median(heights))
heights2.sort()
print("heights2 = ", heights2)
print("Median value of heights2 = ", median(heights2))
```

I have included a sample run below.

```
Mean of heights =   1.68
Mean of heights2 =   1.66
heights =  [1.47, 1.53, 1.57, 1.64, 1.64, 1.68, 1.77, 1.81, 1.84, 1.89]
Median value of heights =   1.66
heights2 =  [1.47, 1.53, 1.57, 1.64, 1.64, 1.68, 1.77, 1.81, 1.84]
Median value of heights2 =   1.64
```

10.4   Functions that return an array

It is possible to write a function that not only passes an array as a parameter, but also returns an array. I will start with a very trivial example.

```
def add5(a) :
    for x in range(len(a)) :
        a[x] += 5
    return a


#   Create initial array with the numbers 1 to 10
num = [1, 2, 3, 4, 5, 6, 7, 8, 9, 10]

b = add5(num)

for x in range(len(b)) :
    print(b[x], "\t", end = "")
```

In this example, it can be seen that array num is passed to the function add5(). The function add5() adds 5 to each of the elements of the array. The modified array is passed as a return value to the function call where it is assigned to the variable b.

A less trivial example would be to use this idea to generate the first 100 Fibonacci numbers. You will recall that the following sequence is made up of Fibonacci numbers.

Fibonacci numbers = 1, 1, 2, 3, 5, 8, 13, 21, 34, ...

And, that the next Fibonacci number can be generated by adding the two previous terms. That is Fib(n+2) = Fib(n) + Fib(n+1).

Note, this can be rewritten so that Fib(n) = Fib(n-2) + Fib(n-1). Here I have just replaced n with n-2. This is the format I will use in the following program.

```
def fib(f) :
    f[0] = 1
    f[1] = 1
    for x in range(2, len(f)) :
        f[x] = f[x-2] + f[x-1]
    return f

numbers = [0] * 100     # Create an array to hold 100 integers

FibSequence = fib(numbers)
print("20th Fibonacci number = ", FibSequence[19])
print("100th Fibonacci number = ", FibSequence[99])
```

The output from this program is as follows.

```
20th Fibonacci number =  6765
100th Fibonacci number =  354224848179261915075
```

This is a very easy program to understand. An array called numbers is created and passed to the function fib() as a parameter. The first two values of this array are both set to 0. I then process the rest of the array using a for loop. Initially I add f[0] and f[1] to obtain f[3] and so on. Finally, when the entire array has been filled with Fibonacci numbers, the entire array is passed to the function call.

10.5 Two-dimensional lists (arrays)

A two-dimensional list is often called a table. An example table is shown below.

1	2	3	4	5
6	7	8	9	10
11	12	13	14	15

You can think of this table as 3 rows of numbers with 5 numbers in each row. We can implement this in Python by creating a list that contains 3 lists that correspond to each row.

```
table = [[1, 2, 3, 4, 5], [6, 7, 8, 9, 10], [11, 12, 13, 14, 15]]
```

We can display the table using the statement `print(table)`. If we do, we just get the following.

```
[[1, 2, 3, 4, 5], [6, 7, 8, 9, 10], [11, 12, 13, 14, 15]]
```

This does not present the table in the way that we would like. It does not have the appearance of being two-dimensional.

We can see that each of the rows can be accessed by using the index operator.

```
>>> table = [[1, 2, 3, 4, 5], [6, 7, 8, 9, 10], [11, 12, 13, 14, 15]]
>>> table[0]
[1, 2, 3, 4, 5]
>>> table[1]
[6, 7, 8, 9, 10]
>>> table[2]
[11, 12, 13, 14, 15]
```

We could extend this idea, by using a for loop to access each row. The code to do this may look like the following.

```
for row in table :
    print(row)
```

and the output would look like this.

```
[1, 2, 3, 4, 5]
[6, 7, 8, 9, 10]
[11, 12, 13, 14, 15]
```

This is better, but it still represents the data in the form of lists. Here we have 3 lists representing the 3 rows in the table.

If we were to get a better representation, we would have to mimic accessing an array in the traditional sense. As well as referring to rows, we would have to talk about columns.

We would also need to refer to the index of the row and column explicitly using a number.

```
for row in range(3) :
    for col in range(5) :
        print(table[row][col], "\t", end = "")
    print()
```

In the outer for loop, there are 3 rows that have index values of 0 to 2. Then, in the inner loop there are 5 columns (col), with index values from 0 to 4. Within the body of the inner for loop, we access all the columns for a given row in table. Each element is separated by a tab. Then before we go to the next row, it is necessary to run `print()`, to make sure we start on the next line.

The output from the above follows.

```
1       2       3       4       5
6       7       8       9       10
11      12      13      14      15
```

I now want to continue with this idea, to create an array that holds the equivalent of the multiplication tables. This time, I do not want to create the list of lists explicitly. I will use the multiplication operator instead.

```
table = [[0] * 10] * 10
```

This creates a two dimensional list that is populated with the value 0 throughout. I can verify this by writing a function to print out this table.

```
def printTable(table, n, m) :
    for row in range(n) :
        for col in range(m) :
            print(table[row][col], "\t", end = "")
        print()
```

I can then run this function with the following function call.

```
printTable(table, 10, 10)
```

I can then overwrite this array and store the products of row * col in the array using the following code.

```
for row in range(10) :
    for col in range(10) :
        table[row][col] = row * col
```

Exercise 10

1. Write a program that will:

   (a) Include a function, that will prompt the user for how many numbers they want to enter. It will then create an array of this size and allow the user to fill it with numbers they have entered at the keyboard. The function will return the array once the numbers have been entered.

   (b) Write a number of other functions that will use this array. This should include functions to calculate and display the minimum, maximum, and average of all numbers stored in the array.

   (c) Include appropriate function calls to test these functions.

2. Write a program that will:

   (a) allow you to enter a number indicating how many Strings you wish to enter at the keyboard

   (b) create an array for storing exactly the number of Strings that you wish

   (c) print out each String in the array together with the length of the string

   (d) compute and print out the average length of the strings entered.

3. Write a program that will create a 2-dimensional 5 × 5 square matrix. It will then compute each value in the array using the formula $value = x^2 + 2y$. You will also be required to write two functions that will process this array. The first will print out the array in a tabular format. The second function will return the sum of all the elements within the array.

Lesson 11: Using Files

11.1 Introduction.

For large amounts of data it is not practical to store the data in memory. The data has to be stored on disk, and the container that holds this data is called a file.

The simplest type of file organization is a text file. A text file is merely a large sequence of characters. It is not unlike text typed in from the keyboard. The main difference is that it can be very much larger. Text files only store text. How this text is interpreted is determined by the program that reads it. Like keyboard input, anything you read from a file is considered to be a string. If you want to change certain characters to numbers, this must be done by explicit type casting.

File processing typically consists of the following basic operations.

1. Open a file. When you open a file, you identify the file you want to open, and whether you want to read from the file, or write to the file. This operation also returns a file object which.

2. Read from file. Reading from a file extracts data from the file to one or more variables in memory.

3. Write to the file. Writing to a file takes values from one or more variables and transfers the values to the file.

4. Close the file. Closing a file makes sure that the read and write operations have been completed. In any case, even if not needed, it is standard practice to close a file once file processing has been completed.

In this section, I will first look at how to open a file. This is achieved by using the `open()` function.

If I want to read from a file, I must open the file in read mode. An example follows.

```
infile = open("myfile.txt", "r")
```

In this example, the file called myfile.txt must exist and be in the current directory. If it does not exist you will get an error message when you try and open it. The second parameter is the file mode. The "r" indicates that we will be reading data from the file.

Now, if I use the variable `infile`, it refers to the file myfile.txt.

If we want to write to a file, we must open the file in write mode. An example follows.

```
outfile = open("myfile2.txt", "w")
```

If the file does not exist, an empty file called myfile2.txt will be created and the file object called outfile, will point to the beginning of the file. Then when I write to the file, this data will be transferred to the file, and the file pointer will point to the end of the data added. If the file does exist, the file will be overwritten without any warning.

Finally, when I have finished the file processing, I should close the file. This is achieved using the `close()` method.

11.2 Reading from a file

I will start by looking at a simple example that reads data from a file and then displays the contents on the screen. I need to create the data file beforehand. I have used notepad for this purpose. The file has been included below.

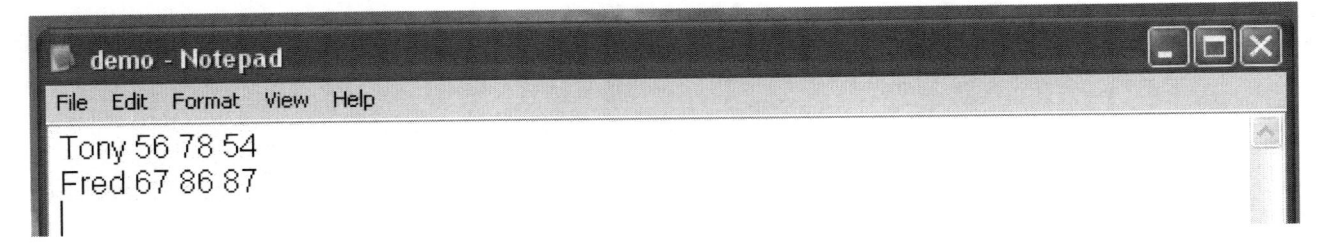

```
demo - Notepad
File  Edit  Format  View  Help
Tony 56 78 54
Fred 67 86 87
```

The following program reads the file and displays the contents.

```
infile = open("demo.txt", "r")
content = infile.read()

print(content)

infile.close()
```

To start with, The open statement is used to open the file demo.txt in read mode. The return value of this function call is a reference to the file. So, whenever we use the name `infile` it refers to the file demo.txt.

The method `read()` needs a file object to call it. The file object is called `infile`. This method reads the entire file and returns its contents. In this instance the contents of the file is stored in the variable called `content`.

You can see that if I print the value of content, I have a display of what is in the file. Finally, you should always close the file.

The output follows.

```
Tony 56 78 54
Fred 67 86 87

>>>
```

Typically when you want to perform file processing, you think of the file as consisting of a number of lines of text. You may want to process the text a line at a time. The method `readline()` can be used for this purpose.

The following program demonstrates this.

```
infile = open("demo.txt", "r")

line1 = infile.readline()
print("Line 1 is \t", line1)
line2 = infile.readline()
print("line 2 is \t", line2)

infile.close()
```

If I run the above program, this is the output.

```
Line 1 is        Tony 56 78 54

line 2 is        Fred 67 86 87

>>>
```

This program opens a file called demo.txt in read mode. It then reads a line of text and stores the result in the variable line1. This is then displayed on the screen using a print statement. This is repeated to obtain the second line of text.

Looking at the output, there is one problem. It appears that an extra line has been printed for each print statement. The reason for this is the fact that each line in the file has a newline character at the end of each line of text. We cannot see it, but have to assume that it is there.

We can remove this newline character by using the rstrip() method. The rstrip() method removes the last character. We can do that as follows.

```
line1 = line1.rstrip()
```

If we add this, and a similar one for line2 before the print statements, the output will be as follows:

```
Line 1 is        Tony 56 78 54
line 2 is        Fred 67 86 87
>>>
```

There is another way that we can access lines of text from within a file. The following program illustrates this.

```
infile = open("demo.txt", "r")

for line in infile :
    line = line.rstrip()
    print(line)

infile.close()
```

The output generated by running this is:

```
Tony 56 78 54
Fred 67 86 87
>>>
```

In this example, a for loop is used to access the file a line at a time. The for loop above can be interpreted as:

For each line in the file :
    Strip the last character from the line
    Print the value of this line

Notice how we do not explicitly have to read from the file using the `read()` or `readline()` methods.

The next problem I want to discuss is how to extract individual data items from each line. In this instance each line consists of a name and 3 numbers. We can extract this information and form a list of 4 items using the `split()` method.

```
infile = open("demo.txt", "r")

for line in infile :
    line = line.rstrip()
    line = line.split()
    print(line)

infile.close()
```

In this case, I have merely added a single line of code.

The statement `line = line.split()` splits a string into a list. You will recall that each line of the file is a sequence of characters, and so is thought of as a string. Within this string, spaces are used as separators by the method `split()`.

```
['Tony', '56', '78', '54']
['Fred', '67', '86', '87']
>>>
```

You can see from the output, that my output is now in the form of two lists. If I were to take one of the lists stored in the variable line, I can easily extract individual data items from it using the indexing operator. I could do that as follows:

```
name = line[0]
num1 = int(line[1])
num2 = int(line[2])
num3 = int(line[3])
```

Notice that I have had to use the `int()` function to convert a string to an integer for 3 of the items in the list. This was necessary because all of the items in the list were strings.

11.3 Writing to a file

Once you have opened a file in write mode you can write strings to it. If I had already opened a file with the statement:

```
outfile = open("hello.txt", "w")
```

I could then use the following write statement to write a string to this file.

```
outfile.write("Hello, World !")
```

If this is all I want to write to the file, I should close the file with:

```
outfile.close()
```

Here, if there is no file called hello.txt, a new file with this name will be created, otherwise the existing file will be overwritten. The string `"Hello, World !"` will be written to it, before the file is closed.

I could then open this file with notepad and find the following.

```
hello - Notepad
File  Edit  Format  View  Help
Hello, World !
```

This appears to be exactly what we intended.

I could continue in this theme. This time I will store a number of strings and the write them to a file. Consider the following program.

```
outfile = open("output.txt", "w")

line1 = "This is the first line"
line2 = "This is the second line"
line3 = "This is the third line"

outfile.write(line1)
outfile.write(line2)
outfile.write(line3)

outfile.close()
```

99

This program writes 3 strings called `line1`, `line2` and `line3` to the file output.txt. But if we check out what is stored in the file by opening the file using notepad, we don't get what we would want.

```
output - Notepad
File  Edit  Format  View  Help
This is the first lineThis is the second lineThis is the third line
```

In particular, all of these strings appear on the same line. To put then on separate lines we need to insert the character \n at the end of each string. This character is the newline character. It will move the cursor to the next line before the next string is written.

To do this I either have to include the newline character at the end of each string.

```
line1 = "This is the first line\n"
```

Or, I could perform a concatenation such as the following after each string assignment.

```
line1 = line1 + "\n"
```

If, I correct this oversight the output from my program will be.

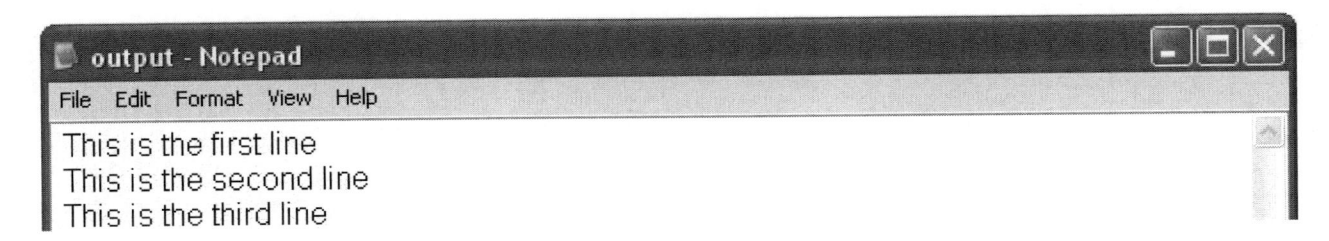

```
output - Notepad
File  Edit  Format  View  Help
This is the first line
This is the second line
This is the third line
```

This is what I had intended to achieve in the first place.

There are other problems to consider if you want to write numbers to a file as well. Let's look at the following program.

```
outfile = open("output.txt", "w")

name = "Tony"
num1 = 56
num2 = 78
num3 = 54

outfile.write(name)
outfile.write(num1)
outfile.write(num2)
outfile.write(num3)

outfile.close()
```

If I run this program, I get the following error message:

```
Traceback (most recent call last):
  File "C:/Documents and Settings/Admin/Desktop/My Python programs/Lesson11/outp
ut2.py", line 10, in <module>
    outfile.write(num1)
TypeError: must be str, not int
>>>
```

What is wrong? The biggest mistake made in this program is the fact that we have tried to write integers to a text file. This is never permissible. You always have to write strings to a text file.

If we had intended to reproduce the first line of the data file we had in section 11.2, we should have converted the numbers to strings. These should then be included in a string using the process of concatenation. A corrected version of this program may look like the following:

```
outfile = open("output.txt", "w")

name = "Tony"
num1 = 56
num2 = 78
num3 = 54

line1 = name + "\t" + str(num1) + "\t" + str(num2) + "\t" + str(num3) + "\n"

outfile.write(line1)

outfile.close()
```

This would have produced output in a sensible format that looks like:

```
output - Notepad
File  Edit  Format  View  Help
Tony    56      78      54
```

Here, I have used a tab as a separator, and have included a newline character at the end. This format will be easy to read if I choose to write a program to read this file. I could have used a space instead, but I think that a tab looks better when a person reads a text file.

11.4 Using functions to process files

In this section, I will be demonstrating how functions can be used in file processing programs. The initial data file is shown below.

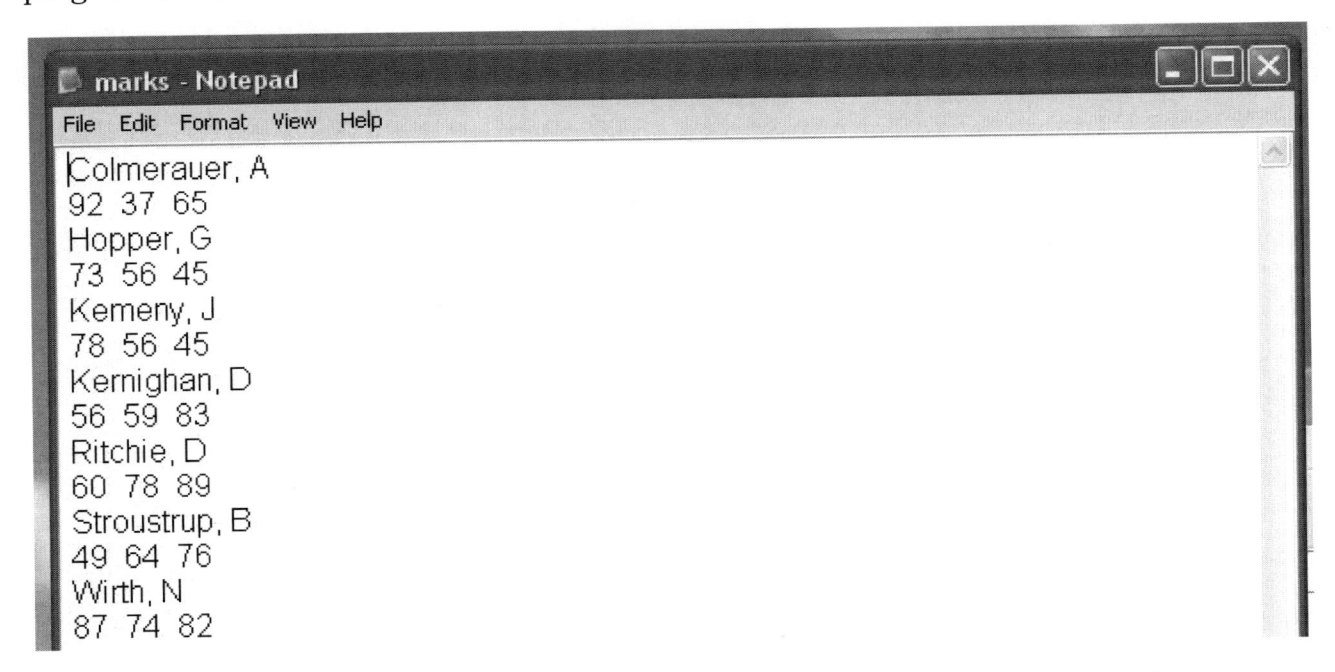

```
marks - Notepad
File  Edit  Format  View  Help
Colmerauer, A
92 37 65
Hopper, G
73 56 45
Kemeny, J
78 56 45
Kernighan, D
56 59 83
Ritchie, D
60 78 89
Stroustrup, B
49 64 76
Wirth, N
87 74 82
```

The aim of the program is to read this data file. You will notice that a record spans two lines. The first line contains a name. The second contains 3 numbers representing 3 marks. The program is supposed to read a record at a time, compute the average of the 3 marks to 2 decimal places, and then write the name and average to another file.

I have only made a start on the program. It will not read the entire file. I have merely written two functions and a small section of code to call these functions to make sure that they work.

The function `readRecord()` will take as a parameter a file object that identifies the file to read from. It reads in two lines of text from the file corresponding to a single record. It will then make sure that the marks are converted to integers. The return value is a list consisting of a name and 3 marks.

The function `writeRecord()` will take as a parameter the record that is intended to be written to the file. It will open the file in append mode, convert the parameter to a suitably formatted string, and then write this string to a file.

An algorithm to describe the program could be:

Open a file for reading
Read a record from the file
Extract numbers from record and compute average
Construct a List with the items to write to the file
Open a file in append mode and write a record to it.

This can be translated to the following program:

```
#    Read two lines from file corresponding to a single record
def readRecord(file) :
    name = file.readline()
    if name != "" :
        name = name.rstrip()
        line2 = file.readline()
        line2 = line2.rstrip()
        line2 = line2.split()
        num1 = int(line2[0])
        num2 = int(line2[1])
        num3 = int(line2[2])
        reclist = [name, num1, num2, num3]
        return reclist
    else :
        return ""

#    Write a single record to end of existing file
def writeRecord(record) :
    outfile = open("grades.txt", "a")
    outString = record[0] + "\t" + str(record[1]) + "\n"
    outfile.write(outString)

infile = open("marks.txt", "r")

record = readRecord(infile)        # Read initial record
while record != "" :
    average = (record[1] + record[2] + record[3]) / 3
    average = round(average, 2)
    outlist = [record[0], average]
    writeRecord(outlist)
    record = readRecord(infile)    # Read next record
```

There are only a few more things that I have to say concerning this program.

The parameter for the function readRecord() is a file object rather than a file name. This is because we only want to open the file for reading once. We then use the reference for the file rather than the file name itself.

The return value from readRecord() is a list. This provides values that are in an appropriate format to be used straight away.

The parameter for writeRecord(), is a list of data items to be written to the file. I could have prepared it ready to write to the file in the form of a string. I decided to do this processing inside the function. The file to be opened from within writeRecord() is opened in append mode. That way, new records get appended to the end of a file rather than the beginning.

The while loop terminates when there are no more records. When this happens an empty string is returned.

Exercise 11

1. Write a program that will be used to create file containing the names of your friends and their telephone numbers.

   (a) This should include a function to enter a name, and telephone number at the keyboard. This function should return a suitably formatted string containing name and number.

   (b) Your function should be called within a while loop, which terminates when you indicate you want to quit.

   (c) After you have called the function to obtain name and telephone number, the string obtained should be written to a file called telNum.txt.

   (d) Check the details of you file by opening it in notepad. Make sure that it is in a suitable format to read.

2. Modify the program in section 6.2 – Quadratic equations revisited. This time, the program will read from a file to obtain the three coefficients.

   (a) Your file should consist of at least 5 lines created using notepad. On each line there should be 3 numbers, corresponding to the coefficients of a quadratic equation – a, b and c. There should be a space or tab to separate each of the numbers.

   (b) Your program should open this file and read all of the lines in the text file that you created using notepad.

   (c) For each line obtained from the file, you will need to extract the 3 numbers before using them to determine the roots.

   (d) Write a function called `quadratic()` that will accept these 3 parameters. The function should first determine whether real roots are possible. If they are the two roots should be returned in a list. If not, the message "No real roots" should be returned in a list.

   (e) Print out the results from the function quadratic in a suitable format.

   (f) You may find the following information useful.

For a given quadratic equation of form $ax^2 + bx + c = 0$. The coefficients are a, b and c. The condition for real roots is $b^2 \leq 4ac$

Lesson 12: A mathematical interlude

12. 1   Standard form

Standard form is used to represent either very large numbers or very small numbers and is based on powers of 10.

I will start by reminding you about powers of 10.

We can for instance, write: $10^2 = 10 \times 10 = 100$, $10^3 = 10 \times 10 \times 10 = 1000$, *and so on.*

If we take a number such as 312000, you can write is as a number times a power of 10. That is: $312000 = 3.12 \times 100000 = 3.12 \times 10^5$. In each case the first number is usually a decimal number, and must have a value between 1 and 10.

Standard form is also called scientific or engineering notation, as it is most commonly used amongst scientists and engineers.

To illustrate how this idea can be used in Python, I will pose a problem to solve.

Einstein's most famous equation is $E = mc^2$. This calculates an amount of energy in Joules given a loss in mass (m) in kg. It uses the speed of light (c).

Given that the speed of light is 299,792,500 ms^{-1}, write a program that calculates and prints out E given that the loss in mass is 2.5g. Represent c as a numeric constant.

```
#    Calculate energy in Joules

c = 2.997925e+8         # constant c, speed of light in metres per second
m = 2.5e-3              # loss of mass in Kg
e = m * c ** 2
print("Energy = ", e, " Joules" )
print("Energy = ", e / 100, " kilo Joules" )
print("Energy = ", e / 1000000, " mega Joules" )
```

The output is as follows.

```
Energy = 224688857640625.0 Joules
Energy = 2246888576406.25 kilo Joules
Energy = 224688857.640625 mega Joules
>>>
```

Notes.

1. Although, I am referring to c as a constant, it is not. You do not have constants in Python. Some people advocate if you want a variable to be treated as a constant, you should use capital letters when you name a constant.

2. The value $299792500 = 2.997925 \times 100000000 = 2.997925 \times 10^8$. In Python this is written as: 2.997925e+8

3. I had to convert the mass in grams to kilograms. There is 1000g in one kg.

12.2 The math module

Python has a standard library that contains numerous modules that can be used in your programs. A module is a collection of related code. This code consists of constants and functions that can be used in your programs. The math module contains various constants and functions for use in mathematics.

We have already used the constant pi, and the function sqrt(). This is where I will start. I will then be selecting a number of features that will be of some familiarity to a GCSE student.

So far, I have suggested that you can use pi in the following manner.

```
import math

r = 5
c = 2 * math.pi * r
a = math.pi * r ** 2
print("Circumference = ", c)
print("Area = ", a)
```

In this example, the import statement makes all of the contents of the math module available to my program. If I want to make use of the constant pi, I need to refer to it as math.pi. This is like saying, use the pi constant from the math module.

There is an alternative to this. I can just select those constants and functions that I want to use from the module. The following program is equivalent to the first example.

```
from math import pi

r = 5
c = 2 * pi * r
a = pi * r ** 2
print("Circumference = ", c)
print("Area = ", a)
```

Here I am just selecting the constant pi from the math module. One advantage of doing this is that is obvious from the above program is the fact that your program code is simpler.

You do not have to restrict yourself to selecting just one item from a module. You can specify a list of items that you want to use.

```
from math import pi, sqrt

print("The value of pi is ", pi)
print("The square root of 2 is ", sqrt(2))
```

I have included the output from this program, so that you can see the number of decimal places you can obtain when using pi or sqrt(). Normally, you would use the round function to obtain a result to 2 or 3 decimal places.

```
The value of pi is  3.141592653589793
The square root of 2 is  1.4142135623730951
>>>
```

12.3 Trigonometry

In this section, we will concern ourselves with the basic trigonometry involving right-angled triangles. We will start with a recap of the trigonometric ratios.

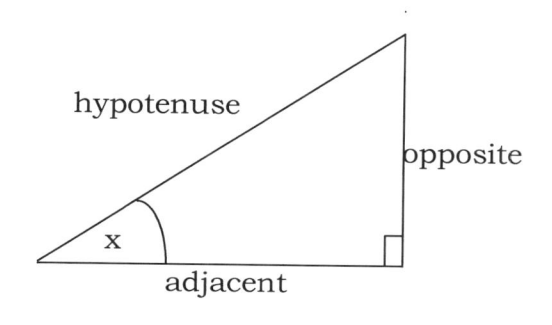

Trigonometric ratios

$$\sin x = \frac{opposite}{hypotenuse}$$

$$\cos x = \frac{adjacent}{hypotenuse}$$

$$\tan x = \frac{opposite}{adjacent}$$

Typically, you would use this information to determine an unknown length given a known length and an angle.

Problem

Determine the length x in the following diagram.

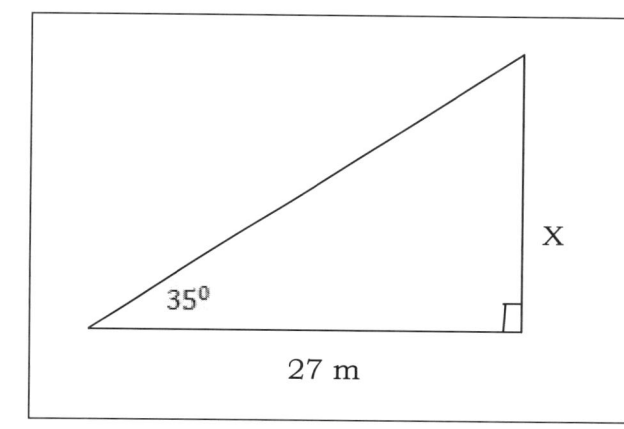

Here you will notice that we will have to use tangent.

$$\frac{x}{27} = \tan 35 \Rightarrow x = 27 \times \tan 35$$

If you were doing this on paper, you would now reach for your calculator to find the tangent of 35 degrees. Then you would multiply this by 27.

Within the math module, you have the following trigonometric functions.

The three trigonometric ratios that have been described can be calculated using the following functions.

sin(x)   returns the sine of an angle given in radians

cos(x)   returns the cosine of an angle given in radians

tan(x)   returns the tangent of an angle given in radians.

When you use a calculator, you can choose whether the angle is in radians or degrees. In the GCSE mathematics, angles are given in degrees, not radians.

You should already know that there are $360°$ in a complete turn. There are 2π radians in a complete turn. So it is a relatively easy matter to convert degrees to radians.

We know that $2\pi \, radians = 360° \Rightarrow 1° = \frac{2\pi}{360} \, radians \Rightarrow x° = \frac{2\pi x}{360} \, radians$

107

So, we could easily perform this calculation to convert an angle in degrees to radians. This is what we could have to do in most other programming languages. Fortunately Python makes this easier for us, by providing two functions that perform a conversion.

degrees(x)   converts x radians to degrees

radians(x)   converts x degrees to radians

We are now in a position to write our first program using trigonometric functions. I will be solving the previous problem.

```
from math import tan, radians

angleDeg = 35
angleRad = radians(angleDeg)
x = 27 * tan(angleRad)
print("The required distance x is ", round(x, 2), " metres")
```

The program does not require any further explanation. I will just show the output.

```
The required distance x is  18.91  metres
>>>
```

Another type of problem involving basic trigonometry, involves calculating an angle given 2 sides of a right-angled triangle.

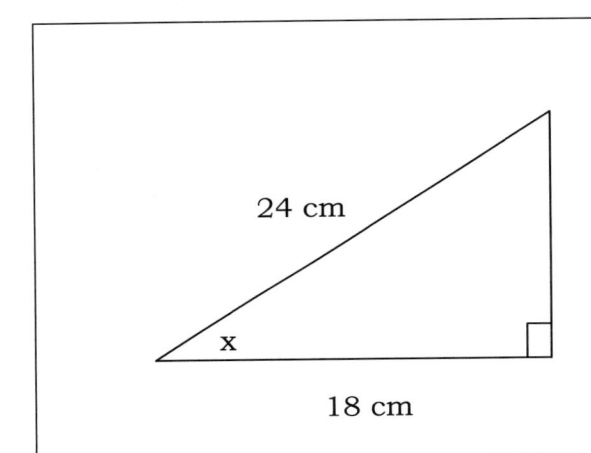

Here we notice that:

$$\cos x = \frac{18}{24} = 0.75$$

$$\Rightarrow x = \cos^{-1} 0.75$$

You will be able to find the inverse cosine button on your calculator ($\cos^{-1}$). This button can be used to calculate the angle x given a cosine of 0.75.

The Python math module provides us with the following inverse trigonometric functions.

asin(x)   returns the angle in radians for the sine given by x

acos(x)   returns the angle in radians for the cosine given by x

atan(x)   returns the angle in radians for the tangent given by x.

I will be demonstrating the use of an inverse trigonometric function, by writing a simple program to solve the above.

The program listing follows.

```
from math import acos, degrees

cosAngle = 18 / 24
angleRad = acos(cosAngle)
angleDeg = degrees(angleRad)

print("Angle x has a value of ", round(angleDeg, 2), " degrees")
```

The output from this is as follows.

```
Angle x has a value of  41.41  degrees
>>>
```

12.4   Random numbers

Probability or chance, is the likelihood that something will happen. There is a probability scale 0 to 1 which is used to measure this likelihood or probability. A value of zero is assigned to an event which is impossible. At the other end of the scale, a value of 1 is only assigned to events which are considered certain. All other events have a probability somewhere between 0 and 1.

In GCSE mathematics, problems in probability often involve tossing coins or throwing dice. If you have a fair coin, it is expected that obtaining heads or tails is equally likely. That is there is a probability of a ½ of obtaining a head. The same is true of a tail.

In the case of throwing a die, for each of the numbers you would expect to obtain a probability of $1/6$. The reason for this, is that there are 6 possible outcomes. As we are assuming that each outcome is equally likely, then the probability of obtaining each number is $1/6$.

We can test these ideas, by throwing a die many times and keep a record of the frequencies for each number. You can then divide the frequencies by the number of times the die is thrown to obtain an average. If the die is unbiased you would expect the results to be close to the theoretical probability. This experimental method of relative frequencies, as described, is not very practical. Imagine how long it would take you to throw a die 1000 times.

Fortunately you do not have to. You can simulate throwing a dice by using random numbers. Python, like many other languages, has the capability of generating pseudorandom numbers. The prefix pseudo, suggests that the random numbers are artificial or fake. This is the case, but the numbers generated are a good approximation of random numbers.

The random class within the Python standard library contains many functions related to random numbers. We will only be looking at a couple of these.

I intend to write a program, to simulate throwing a die. If you throw a die a small number of times, your averages will not be very close to what is expected theoretically. But, as you increase the number of throws your values will get closer.

In the next program, I will use the function `randrange()`. This function returns an integer in the range specified.

So, for instance, a function call `randrange(6)` will return an integer in the range 0 to 5. To simulate a die, we will need to add one to this value. If we do this, we will obtain numbers in the range 1 to 6. The following program illustrates this.

```
from random import randrange

def throwDice(n) :
    #   Initialize counts
    c1 = 0; c2 = 0; c3 = 0; c4 = 0; c5 = 0; c6 = 0

    for x in range(n) :
        num = randrange(6) + 1
        if num == 1 :
            c1 += 1
        elif num == 2 :
            c2 += 1
        elif num == 3 :
            c3 += 1
        elif num == 4 :
            c4 += 1
        elif num == 5 :
            c5 += 1
        elif num == 6 :
            c6 += 1

    diceList = [c1, c2, c3, c4, c5, c6]
    return diceList

num = 10000
freq = throwDice(num)
print(freq)
print("Frequencies")
for x in range(len(freq)) :
    print(freq[x], "\t", end = "")
print()
print("averages")
for x in range(len(freq)) :
    print(freq[x] / num, "\t", end = "")
```

The output from running this program follows.

```
[1688, 1666, 1623, 1744, 1610, 1669]
Frequencies
1688    1666    1623    1744    1610    1669
averages
0.1688  0.1666  0.1623  0.1744  0.161   0.1669
>>>
```

This program uses a function called `throwDice()`. This function takes a parameter n that indicates how many times the die is to be thrown. At the top of the function, there are 6 variables used to maintain a count of the frequencies of each possible number. Initially these counts are set to zero.

There follows a for loop, that repeats n times. Each time it loops, a random number is generated in the range 1 to 6. This value is tested using an if statement. Depending on the value of the number, one of the counters will be incremented by 1.

A list called `diceList` is used to store the 6 frequencies. It is this list that the function returns.

Using this list, it is an easy matter to display the frequencies and averages. Also, you can edit the program to change the value of num. This allows you to run the program many times with different numbers of throws.

Random numbers feature a lot in Statistics/Probability and other branches of mathematics. One such application is numerical integration. A simple example of this is given below to estimate the value of Pi. The technique being used is called a Monte Carlo simulation.

Monte Carlo simulation

Imagine you had a square dartboard with a quadrant drawn on it as shown. Now imagine that you have to throw the darts blind folded, but only count the darts that end up in the board. The idea is to throw a large number of darts into the dart board and record the frequencies that darts land in region A and region B. Obviously, this is not practical, as it will take far too long. Instead we will simulate this using random numbers.

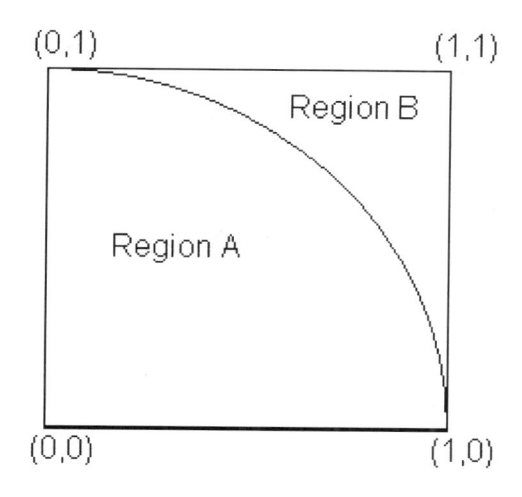

I intend to use the `random()` function for this simulation. This function returns a floating point number in the range 0 to 1. The idea is to obtain two random numbers, x and y each time. This pair of numbers is to represent the position of where the dart lands on the board. To land inside region A, $x^2 + y^2 \le 1$. We know this because for any point (x, y) on the circle, we can apply Pythagoras theorem. As the radius of this circle is 1, then the inequality I have given must hold if the dart is to land inside the quadrant.

The area of the quadrant of the circle is assumed to be proportional to the ratio of random points falling inside Region A to the total number of random points falling inside the square (Regions A + B).

We know that the area of this square is 1. We also know that the area of the quadrant is a quarter the area of a circle = $\frac{\pi r^2}{4}$. In this case the area of the quadrant is $\frac{\pi}{4}$.

So, the ratio of A : (A + B) will give you a value for $\frac{\pi}{4}$.

A program to do this follows.

```
from random import random

num = 10000              # Number of darts to throw
freqA = 0
freqB = 0
for n in range(num) :
    x = random()         # x coordinate
    y = random()         # y coordinate
    if x ** 2 + y ** 2 <= 1 :
        freqA += 1
    else :
        freqB += 1

myPiEstimate = 4 * freqA / num
print("Estimate for Pi is ", myPiEstimate)
```

And the output for a sample run is as follows.

```
Estimate for Pi is  3.1556
>>> 
```

Obviously, if we were to increase the value of num, the value obtained would be more accurate. Also, I should point out that if I run this program many times without changing anything, the result obtained would be different each time. We are dealing with random numbers; nothing is totally predictable.

12.5 Numerical solution of a cubic equation

Iteration is a numerical method for solving equations, which would otherwise be difficult to solve. It usually involves rearranging the equation and transforming the equation into an iterative formula or recurrence relation.

The following is a typical GCSE mathematics calculator paper question.

Show that the cubic equation $x^3 - 3x + 1 = 0$ can be rewritten to form the iterative formula

$$x_{n+1} = \frac{-1}{x_n^2 - 3}$$

And, given an initial solution $x_1 = 0.5$, find a root to this equation that is accurate to 3 decimal places.

Starting with $x^3 - 3x + 1 = 0$, we can rearrange this to: $x(x^2 - 3) + 1 = 0$

$\Rightarrow x(x^2 - 3) = -1 \Rightarrow x = \dfrac{-1}{x^2 - 3}$

We can now rewrite this in the form of an iterative formula as follows:

$$x_{n+1} = \dfrac{-1}{x_n^2 - 3}$$

A first iteration with a calculator, will give you $x_2 = \dfrac{-1}{(0.5)^2 - 3} = 0.36363636\ldots\ldots$

I now include a completed program to solve this.

```
#    Numerical solution for a cubic
import math

count = 0
x1 = 0.5
d = 0.1       # Used on first test in while loop

while d > 0.0005 :
    x2 = -1 / (x1 ** 2 - 3)
    d = math.fabs(x2 - x1)
    x1 = x2
    count += 1
    print(x2)

print('Approx root is ', round(x1, 3))
print('It took ', count, ' iterations')
#    Substitute in root to see how close to zero
f = x1 ** 3 - 3 * x1 + 1
print ('f is ', f)
```

The output from this program will be:

```
0.36363636363636365
0.34870317002881845
0.347414494526611
0.34730625478031896
Approx root is  0.347
It took  4  iterations
f is  -2.6116179240309734e-05
>>>
```

The while loop tests for a difference between two adjacent solutions which is denoted by d. We are only interested in positive differences, that is why the math function `fabs()` is used. The function `fabs()` returns a positived value, despite the fact that x2-x1 may be negative. A difference of 0.0005 is chosen because we want the answer accurate to 3 decimal places.

After finding the absolute difference, x1 is set to the value of x2. For the next iteration x2 will be calculated using the value of x1. This is a very old programmers trick to reuse variables.

A count is maintained, so that we know how many iterations took place to arrive at our result. There is a redundant print statement after the statement that increments count. This can be removed, but it is useful for debugging purposes.

12.6 Very large prime numbers

A number is prime if it has exactly 2 factors, 1 and itself. According to this defintion, 1 is not prime, because it has a single factor.

Supposed I were to ask you what the 100th or 1000th prime number was. How would you go about this? Lets start with the prime numbers with a value less that 100. You could write a for loop, which tests all of the numbers in the range 2 to 100. But, to get this right, the logic is very difficult using this approach and very inefficient.

I am going to suggest that we use a method developed by the ancient Greeks. It is called the sieve of Eratosthenes. To illustate this, I have created a table of the first 100 numbers and will be using this to find primes less than 100.

The idea is, starting with 2, cross out all of the numbers that are divisble by 2, excluding 2 itself. Then continue with 3 etc. There is no need going beyond 10. You can see the result, of me crossing out numbers that are divisible by 2. You keep doing this by crossing out the numbers divisible by 3 etc. Then, when you have finished, what you are left with is the prime numbers. You can of course leave out 1, as this is not prime by definition.

1	2	3	4̶	5	6̶	7	8̶	9	1̶0̶
11	1̶2̶	13	1̶4̶	15	1̶6̶	17	1̶8̶	19	2̶0̶
21	2̶2̶	23	2̶4̶	25	2̶6̶	27	2̶8̶	29	3̶0̶
31	3̶2̶	33	3̶4̶	35	3̶6̶	37	3̶8̶	39	4̶0̶
41	4̶2̶	43	4̶4̶	45	4̶6̶	47	4̶8̶	49	5̶0̶
51	5̶2̶	53	5̶4̶	55	5̶6̶	57	5̶8̶	59	6̶0̶
61	6̶2̶	63	6̶4̶	65	6̶6̶	67	6̶8̶	69	7̶0̶
71	7̶2̶	73	7̶4̶	75	7̶6̶	77	7̶8̶	79	8̶0̶
81	8̶2̶	83	8̶4̶	85	8̶6̶	87	8̶8̶	89	9̶0̶
91	9̶2̶	93	9̶4̶	95	9̶6̶	97	9̶8̶	99	1̶0̶0̶

In fact, if you think about it there is no need to divide by all the numbers in the range 2 to 10. You can leave out 4, 6, 8, and 10 because these are composite numbers. So, for the prime numbers less than 100, you only need to divide by the prime numbers 2, 3, 5, and 7.

My idea, is to start with a small list of prime numbers [2, 3, 5, 7], and use this to build up a bigger list of prime numbers.

I will initally create a list of numbers between 10 and 100. Any number in this list that is divisible by any of the numbers in my initial list of prime numbers, cannot be prime. So, I need to remove them from the list. By the time I have finished, any number that remains, must be prime.

I can now concatenate the original list of primes with the remaining numbers in this list to obtain a bigger list of primes.

I can then build bigger lists of numbers, which I can test for primality with my larger list of primes.

There follows a completed program that allows me to determine the 100th, 1000th, and 10000th prime number.

```
#    Calculate large primes

def createNumbers (n) :
    numbers = []
    for number in range (n, n ** 2 + 1) :
        numbers.append (number)
    return numbers

def createPrimes (primes, numbers) :
    for prime in primes :
        for number in numbers :
            if number % prime == 0 and number in numbers :
                numbers.remove (number)
    primes = primes + numbers
    return primes

primes = [2, 3, 5, 7 ]                          # Initial list of primes < 10
numbers = createNumbers (10)
primes = createPrimes (primes, numbers)         # primes < 100

numbers = createNumbers (300)
primes = createPrimes (primes, numbers)         # primes < 900000

print ("Number of primes generated is ", len (primes))
print ("One hundreth prime number is ", primes [99])
print ("One thousandth prime number is ", primes [999])
print ("Ten thousandth prime number is ", primes [9999])
```

```
Number of primes generated is  10610
One hundreth prime number is  773
One thousandth prime number is  8269
Ten thousandth prime number is  84059
>>>
```

The first function has a single parameter n, and creates a list of numbers in the range n to n^2. So, if n = 10, I will obtain a list of numbers from 10 to 100. This function uses the list method `append()` to add a number to the end of the list each time. You could have created a fixed length array, and then update the numbers using a for loop.

The function `createPrimes()` takes 2 parameters, the name of the list of primes, and the name of the list of numbers. There is a nested for loop. The outer for loop takes each of the prime numbers in turn. The inner for loop takes each of the numbers in turn. This allows us to divide each of the numbers in the list by each of the prime numbers. Those that give a remainder of zero, cannot be prime, so should be removed from the list.

There is an added precaution. You cannot remove a number from a list if it is not there. It may have been removed earlier. For this reason, it is essential that you check that the number is in the list before you try and remove it.

I did not print out the list of prime numbers, it is far too large. You can however extract individual prime numbers using the index operator. This has been done.

This algorithm is not terribly efficient and takes several minutes to run. Also, had I tried to create a much larger list of prime numbers, I would have had problems with insufficient memory.

Exercise 12

1. Convert the following numbers to standard form. Then write an assignment statement using Python that assigns the number in stardard form to a variable.

    (a) 234000   (b) 0.0045   (c) four hundred million   (d) two thousandths

2. Calculate a value for the mass of the earth given the following data. Display the result in kg and metric tonnes.

    Radius of earth = 6.371 km, average density = 3.93 g/cm^3. You can assume that the earth is a regular sphere, and that the volume of this is given by: $v = \frac{4}{3}\pi r^3$.
    You are recommended to convert all of these values to SI units. That is distance should be in metres (m), mass should be kg, density should be in kg/m^3.

3. A kite, with a string of 30 metres length has been caught in a tree that is 20 metres away. The end of the string is currently touching the ground and is taut. What is the angle of elevation that the string makes with the horizontal? Draw a diagram to represent this problem. Then write a Python program to solve it.

4. Use random numbers to generate random 5 letter words. Write a function that will generate a random 5 digit word. Call this function 25 times and display the results in a table that consists of 5 rows with 5 words in each row.

5. Show that the equation $x^3 - x^2 - 7 = 0$ can be rearranged to form the recurrence relation:

    $$x_{n+1} = \sqrt[3]{x_n^2 + 7}$$

    Use this to determine the value of one of the roots of the equation to 3 decimal places given an initial value of $x_1 = 2.0$.

Lesson 13: Algorithms, flowcharts and pseudo-code

13.1 Flowcharts

A flowchart is a very visual form for representing an algorithm. In essence, flowcharts have been used prior to the emergence of computers and programming.

I include an example below that is more likely to appear in a biology book in some form. It is a flowchart to classify types of vertebrate.

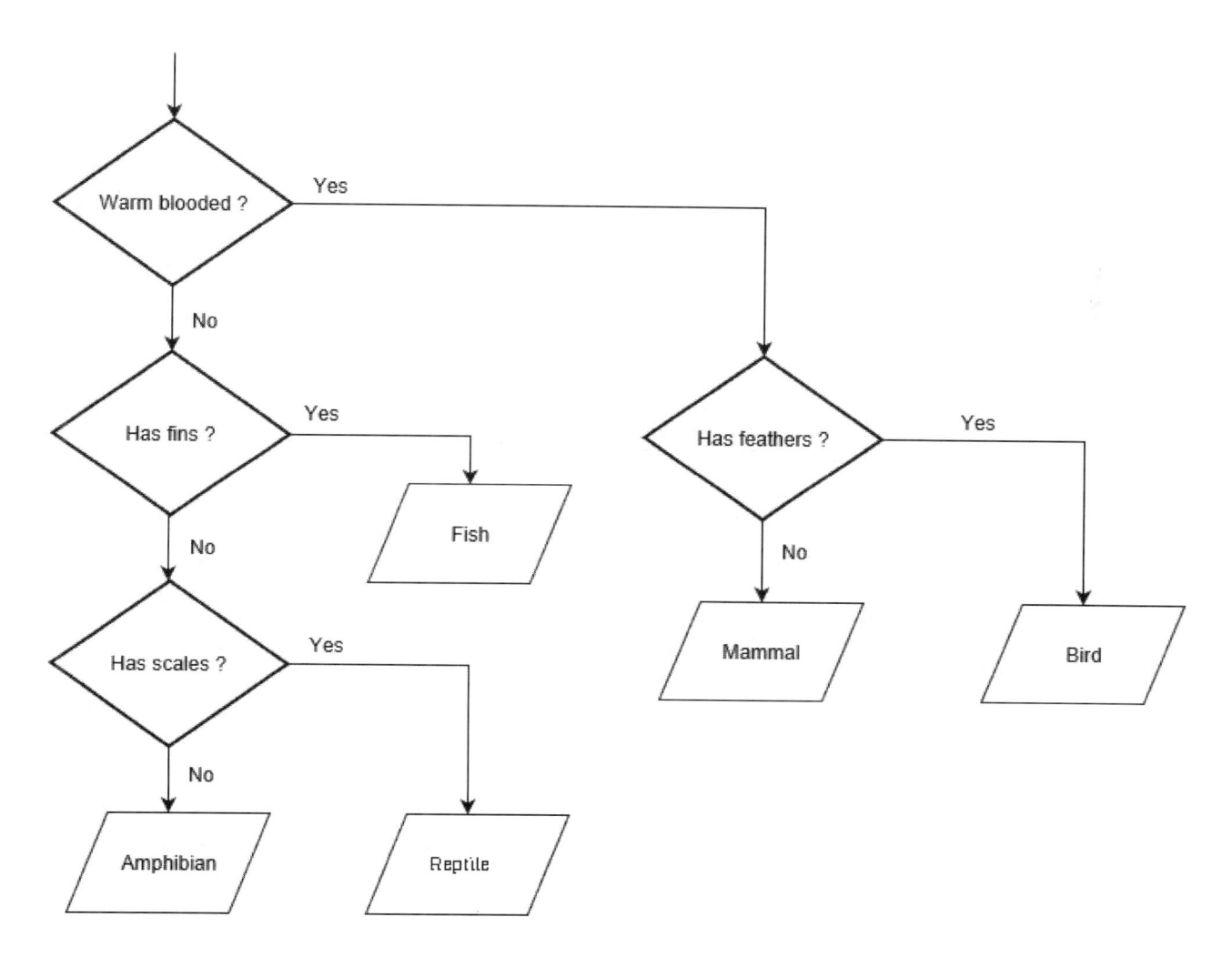

This classification key is often referred to as a **dichotomous key** because of the fact that there are always two choices. For each decision box, there are always two choices. Starting at the top, a vertebrate is either cold-blooded or warm-blooded. This process of asking questions, and having a choice of two possible answers, gives us a means to work out what type of vertebrate we have.

The flowchart illustrated above is more likely to be represented in a non-graphical form that is in the form of questions that lead to the correct answer.

The format of a dichotomous key is most likely to appear like this.

1. Cold blooded 2
    Warm blooded 4

2. Has fins ....Fish
    Has 4 limbs 3

3. Has scales ....Reptile
    No scales ....Amphibian

4. Has feathers ....Bird
    Fur, no feathers ....Mammal

In the days, of unstructured programming, when flowcharts were fashionable, you could possibly see a program to implement the above as follows.

```
10    IF coldblooded = T   GOTO 30
20    IF coldblooded = F   GOTO 70
30    IF fins = T PRINT "Fish" : END
40    IF fins = F GOTO 50
50    IF scales = T PRINT "Reptile" : END
60    IF scales = F PRINT "Amphibian" : END
70    IF feathers = T PRINT "Bird" : END
80    IF feathers = F PRINT "Mammal" : END
```

The above program is unstructured and looks like it has been written in an early form of the BASIC programming language. Note the use of line numbers which enabled you to make use of the goto statement. This type of programming has been discouraged since the 1960s.

I once made the mistake of including flowcharts in one of my pieces of coursework in the 1980s. I received the comment, *"Use of flowcharts quite unnecessary and perhaps indicating a misguided approach to programming"*.

In hindsight, I have to agree. Flowcharts are useful for representing low-levels of abstraction. So, they are still useful for explaining programs in a low-level language such as an assembly language. But, they are not useful at all to explain programs written in a programming language that uses high-level structures such as selection statements and iteration statements etc.

So, why are the exam boards so keen for you to use them to document your programs? I am afraid I cannot answer that question. All I can say is that flowcharts appear in the written exam papers, and it is suggested that you use flowcharts in your programming coursework. So, whatever the justification for using them, you need to know about them, precisely because you will see them in past exam papers and may have to use them in your coursework.

13.2 Flowcharts and pseudo-code for programming constructs

In this section, I will be using flowcharts and pseudo-code to help explain various programming constructs that we have seen previously.

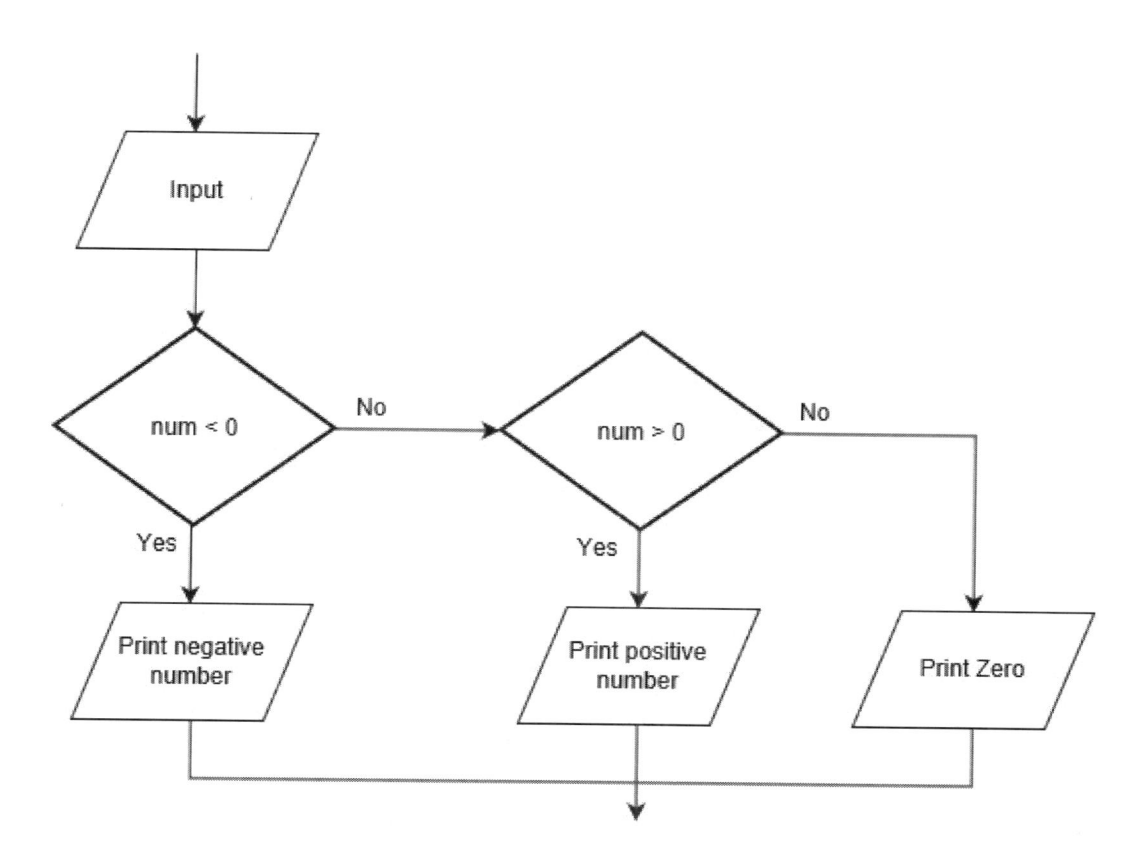

Above, we have an if statement that appeared in a program earlier. This time it is represented as a flowchart. Initially, a number is input. In the first decision box, we are asking whether the number is less than zero. If it is, follow the arrow down, and Print "negative number". Otherwise, take the arrow to the right which takes you to another decision box that poses the question, is the number greater than zero. I am sure that you have understood this by now, I don't need to complete the explanation.

This algorithm can also be described clearly using pseudo-code. Below, I am using a pseudo-code that most closely resembles that advocated by AQA, and I have included corresponding Python code.

```
num ← userInput
IF num < 0 THEN
    OUTPUT "Negative number"
ELSE IF num > 0 THEN
    OUTPUT "Positive number"
ELSE
    OUTPUT "Zero"
END IF
```

```
num = int(input(num))
if num < 0 :
    print("Negative number"
elif num > 0 :
    print("Positive number")
else :
    print("Zero"
```

I should note that the pseudo-code used by AQA most closely resembles that of programs written in QBASIC.

I will now look at an algorithm that uses the for loop. You can see why the for loop is often referred to as a loop with a counter.

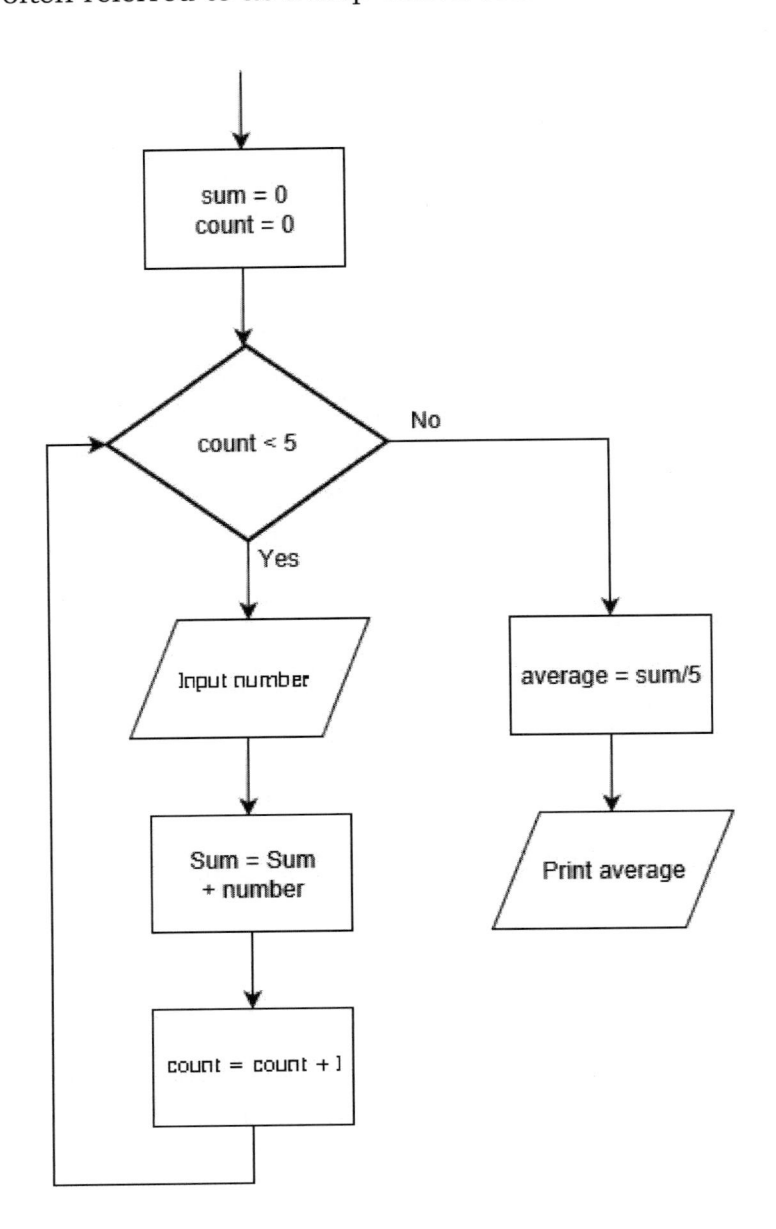

```
sum = 0
count = 0

count < 5 ?
  Yes → Input number
        Sum = Sum + number
        count = count + 1
        (loop back)
  No  → average = sum/5
        Print average
```

Initially, there is a process box, which initializes the variables sum and count. Next, the value of count is tested. If the value is less that 5, you go down the flowchart and input a number. This number is added to the current value of sum, and the value of count is incremented by 1 to indicate how many times round the loop.

Once the variable count reaches 5, the loop terminates. The average is worked out and the result printed. Some of this detail is hidden when you use a for statement to implement this algorithm.

`Sum ← 0`
`FOR count ← 0 TO 5`
`    number ← userInput`
`    sum ← sum + number`
`END FOR`
	`sum = 0`
	`for count in range(5)`
	`    number = int(input())`
	`    sum += number`

Note, if I use a for construct the counter is automatically incremented for me. This is true of both the pseudo-code and the Python code.

Below I am comparing a general for loop with that of a general while loop

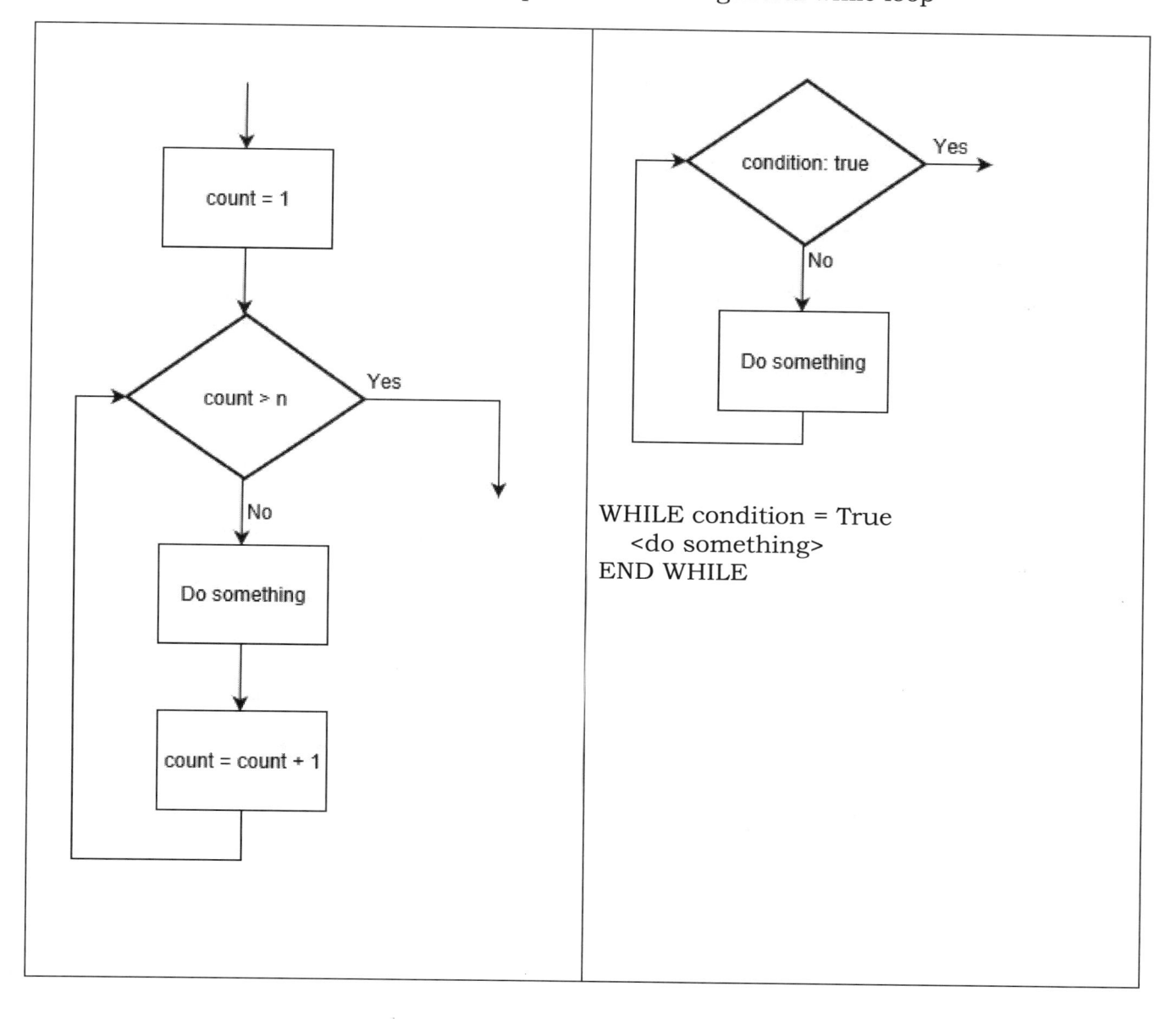

[Flowchart: for loop on left showing count = 1, then decision count > n (Yes exits, No goes to Do something, then count = count + 1, loops back to decision). On right: while loop showing decision condition: true (Yes exits, No goes to Do something, loops back).]

WHILE condition = True
    <do something>
END WHILE

The main difference is that I do not need to maintain a counter to count how many times the program will loop. While loops generally terminate when some other condition has been reached.

13.3 Program design with Structure charts

At some time in your course you will need to hand in a coursework which requires a little more documentation than a program listing and a couple of screen dumps. In these notes, we will be presenting the development of a single program - starting with a description of the problem and ending with a working program that has been tested.

Such a coursework may contain the following components:

1. **A statement of the problem** (or specification).

    In simple terms, you need to know what the project is about. If you choose your own assignment, it is up to you to provide the specification.

2. **An Analysis.**

    This is your interpretation of the problem. You are supposed to explain the problem in such a way, to show that you understand what is required, and suggest how it could be attempted. An analysis often involves research. You could look for similar problems and discuss how they relate to the problem that you have to solve.

3. **Design.**

    A design is a plan of how you are going to solve the problem. In this particular case, how you are going to write a Python program.

    It is typically made up of a number of components such as:
    - Design of Input. e.g. Screen layout and data entry
    - Design of Output e.g. Output to screen and /or printer
    - Data Storage
    - Design of the program

4. **Implementation**
    This means writing the program and getting it to work. Proof of this stage is often satisfied by providing a listing of the program, and some of the output from the program in the form of a screen dump.

5. **Testing**

    The first criterion for testing a program is to ensure that it produces the correct results in all situations. This often involves providing test data to see if you get the results that you would expect to get. Another thing to consider is the ease of use to a user.

6. Evaluation of the System

Here you have to discuss your solution, how you think the program met its requirements, and improvements you could make.

In this section of the book, I will only be looking at the specification, analysis, and design.

Specification

The following is an example of a problem that could be set for your coursework.

A local company wants to make a start at automating their payroll system. Currently the wage packets are made up individually. They get paid in cash and have a pay receipt that details hours worked, rate of pay, overtime and gross pay etc.

(a) Assuming a basic week is 37.5 hours and that any time over this is to be treated as overtime which is to be paid as 1.5 times the standard rate. Write a program that will accept input from the user for :

   Employee name, hours worked, rate of pay

(b) The program will calculate :-

```
overtime worked
basic salary   (not including overtime)
overtime pay
gross pay (basic salary + overtime pay)
```

(c) The program will display each of the values input from the keyboard, together with the items calculated above.

Add comments to document the program, and ensure that the program is readable by including appropriate indentation and spacing.

Analysis

This would appear to be a very simple program which requires the calculation of pay for a single employee. This could easily be computed using a calculator as follows:

Assume rate = 10.00 and hours = 45

basic pay = £37.5 × 10 = £375
overtime = 45 - 37.5 = 7.5 (hours worked - 37.5)
overtime pay = 7.5 × £10.00 × 1.5 = £112.50
gross pay = basic pay + overtime pay = £375.00 + £112.50 = 487.50

Here we assume that we have to subtract 37.5 from the number of hours worked to obtain the number of hours to be paid at the overtime rate. But, what if the number of hours worked is less than 37·5?

We can conclude from this that if hours worked > 37.5 then there is overtime to be paid, otherwise there is no overtime.

There is a more difficult problem to resolve. If someone works less than the standard week (less that 37.5 hours) should they have their basic weekly pay reduced. The specification is not clear here - so it is open to interpretation.

Design

A program design usually starts with the programmer considering screen layout for input and output. The programming itself is usually very easy when you know where things are to appear on the screen. Plan it on paper first. Then write a few test programs to try out the layout. Do this for each of the screen layouts you intend to have in your program. Keep your screen designs and the program fragments that can generate such screens.

Another consideration is that of storage. In this program, we are only going to be using variables to store data. It is common practice to produce a table listing all variables. In this table you will describe the type of data that can be stored, and what it is going to be used for. Such a table is called a **data dictionary** by some. Programs using large amounts of data will probably use files. In this case, it will be necessary to design a **record structure**.

We are now in a position to start designing the program proper.

One method of designing a program is called **Top down Design** using a technique called **Stepwise Refinement**. The idea is to start with a very general description of the program. This description typically only has a few components. Then take each of these components in turn and provide more detail (add refinement). This often means that the components themselves get broken into smaller components, until such a time that the components are detailed enough that they can be translated into Python code.

This design method can be represented using either **pseudo-code** or a more graphical, means such as **structure-charts**. A well known methodology that uses structure charts is called **Jackson Structured programming** (JSP). It was designed by Michael Jackson, but not the one who use to sing and dance, nor the Michael Jackson who is a world famous expert on beer.

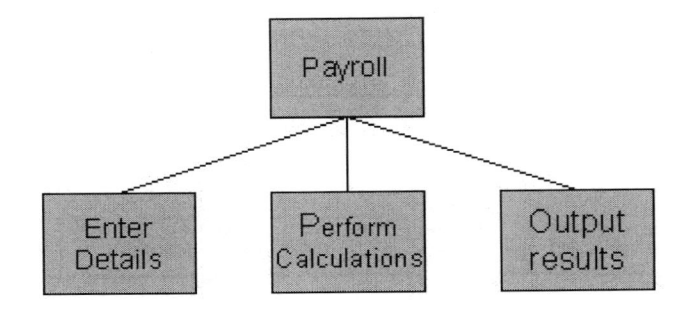

1st level design (pseudocode)

1. Enter details
2. Perform calculations
3. Output results

Structure chart

```
                Payroll
       /           |           \
   Enter       Perform        Output
  Details    Calculations     results
```

2nd level design

    Enter details
1.1 Enter employees name
1.2 Enter number of hours worked
1.3 Enter hourly rate of pay
    Perform calculations
2.1 Calculate overtime
2.2 Calculate basic pay
2.3 Calculate gross pay
    Output results
3.1 Display Employee name
3.2 Display number of hours worked
3.3 Display Hourly rate of pay
3.4 Display Basic pay
3.5 Display number of hours overtime worked
3.6 Display overtime pay earned
3.7 Display gross pay

A corresponding structure chart can easily be drawn. This has been left as an exercise.

13.4 Jackson structured programming

In this chapter we will look at a particular program design methodology called Jackson Structured Programming or just JSP in short. This methodology uses structure charts and uses the principle of stepwise refinement. It also holds that all programs should be built from the three fundamental structured control-constructs – sequences, selection and iteration. The JSP structure charts are applicable to both data and programs. The structure charts for the data should show correspondences with the structure chart of the program that is to process this data.

We will start by looking at how the 3 basic control constructs are depicted using JSP.

Construct	JSP Structure chart	JSP pseudocode	program code

Sequence	A → B, C, D	A. seq
		  do B
		  do C
		  do D
		A. end
			B
			C
			D

Selection	A → B°, C° ≡ A→B° _0 A→B°	A. select
		  do B
		A. or
		  do C
		A. end
			if <condition> :
			  B
			else :
			  C
			
			if <condition> :
			  B

Iteration	A → B*	A. iter
		  do B
		A. end
			while <cond> :
			  B

I will now illustrate these design constructs with the following example. Write a program to draw two types of box as illustrated below.

Extended ASCII characters required to draw boxes

Single line

218   196   191
 ┌   ─   ┐

192   179   217
 └   │   ┘

Double line

201   205   187
 ╔   ═   ╗

200   186   188
 ╚   ║   ╝

126

You will notice the required graphics characters and their respective ASCII codes have been included.

We will produce a design to produce the double line box. An Initial design would probably look like this.

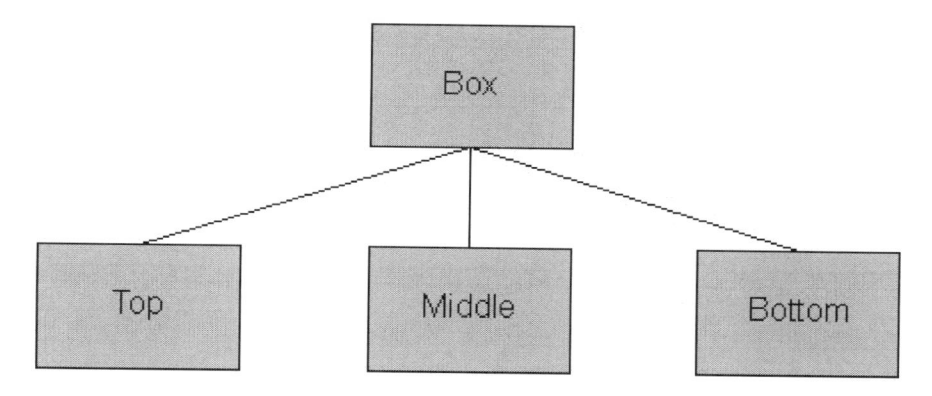

```
              ┌─────┐
              │ Box │
              └──┬──┘
         ┌───────┼───────┐
      ┌──┴──┐ ┌──┴───┐ ┌─┴────┐
      │ Top │ │Middle│ │Bottom│
      └─────┘ └──────┘ └──────┘
```

As it was stated before, JSP uses the idea of stepwise refinement. Now all we have to do is to expand the above design. We will start by examining how a first line of the box is composed. This we have called top.

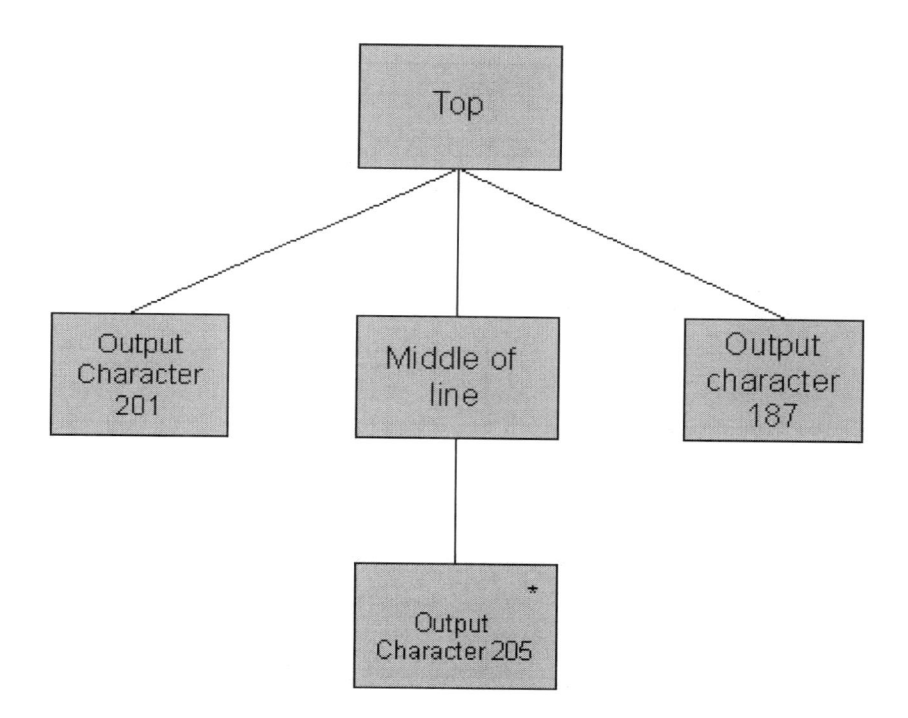

```
                  ┌─────┐
                  │ Top │
                  └──┬──┘
         ┌───────────┼───────────┐
   ┌─────┴────┐ ┌────┴────┐ ┌────┴─────┐
   │  Output  │ │Middle of│ │  Output  │
   │Character │ │  line   │ │character │
   │   201    │ │         │ │   187    │
   └──────────┘ └────┬────┘ └──────────┘
                     │ *
               ┌─────┴──────┐
               │   Output   │
               │Character 205│
               └────────────┘
```

The second level design for top consists of outputting the first character, the middle-part of the line, and the last character in the line. The process "Middle of line" is an iteration, or repetition of outputting character 205.

The middle part of the box can be represented as follows:

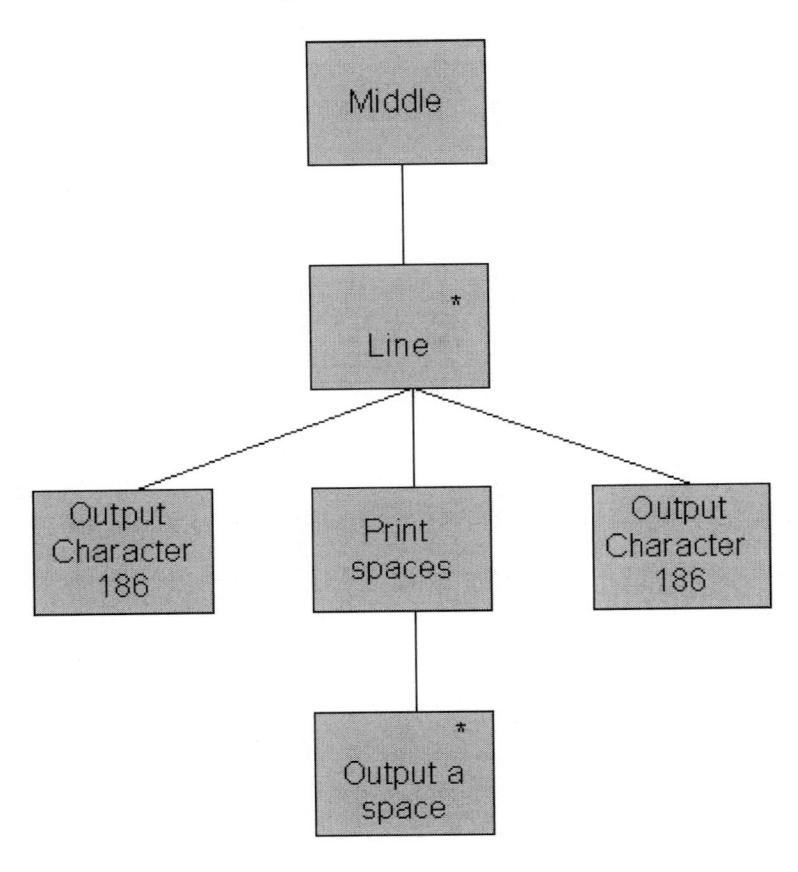

```
                    ┌──────────┐
                    │  Middle  │
                    └────┬─────┘
                         │
                    ┌────┴─────┐  *
                    │   Line   │
                    └────┬─────┘
           ┌─────────────┼─────────────┐
     ┌─────┴────┐  ┌─────┴────┐  ┌─────┴────┐
     │  Output  │  │  Print   │  │  Output  │
     │ Character│  │  spaces  │  │ Character│
     │   186    │  │          │  │   186    │
     └──────────┘  └─────┬────┘  └──────────┘
                         │
                    ┌────┴─────┐  *
                    │ Output a │
                    │  space   │
                    └──────────┘
```

The second level design for bottom is similar to top. For completeness is included below.

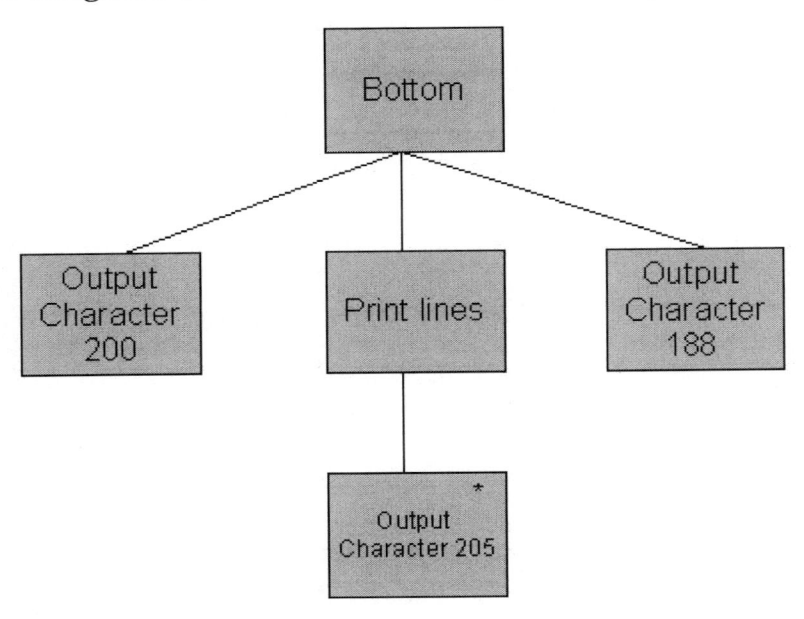

```
                    ┌──────────┐
                    │  Bottom  │
                    └────┬─────┘
           ┌─────────────┼─────────────┐
     ┌─────┴────┐  ┌─────┴────┐  ┌─────┴────┐
     │  Output  │  │          │  │  Output  │
     │ Character│  │Print lines│ │ Character│
     │   200    │  │          │  │   188    │
     └──────────┘  └─────┬────┘  └──────────┘
                         │
                    ┌────┴─────┐  *
                    │  Output  │
                    │Character 205│
                    └──────────┘
```

Exercise 13

1. Implement this design in the form of a short Python program.

2. Look for examples of flowcharts that you can implement in the form of pseudo-code and Python program code.

Lesson 14:   Searching and sorting

14.1   Linear search

In this section we are going to look at some more advanced applications of arrays. This will give you an introduction to the topic of searching and sorting data.

The simplest type of searching technique is called a **Linear Search**. In simple terms this means starting at the beginning of an array and scanning the array one element at a time until the required item is found. The main loop to access the array might look like this:

```
i = 0
while i < len(num) - 1 and num[i] != x
    i = i + 1                   # Skip past unwanted items
```

We now need to test which of the two conditions terminated the loop.

```
if num[i] == x :
    print("Item found at location ", i)
else :
    print("Item not found")
```

This is an effective method to search for items in an array if the array is very small. But for large arrays it would be very slow as the number of comparisons and hence the time taken is proportional to the number of elements in the array.

For completeness, I have written a function called lSearch(), which carries out a linear search.

```
def lsearch(a, x) :
   i = 0
   while i < len(a) - 1 and a[i] != x :
       i += 1                       # skip uneanted items
   if a[i] == x :
       return i                     # number is found at i
   else :
       return - 1                   # indicate failure

#   Test function
numbers = [33, 42, 23, 76, 45, 32, 27, 23, 49, 22]
num = int(input("Enter a whole number : "))

result = lsearch(numbers, num)
if result != -1 :
   print(num, " was found at position with index value ", result)
else :
   print("Number was not found")
```

14.2 Binary search

A faster method to search for an item in an array is called a Bisection Search. For this to work the items in the array must be sorted.

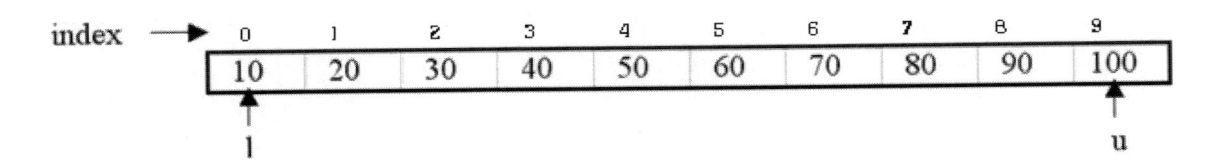

```
index →    0    1    2    3    4    5    6    7    8    9
         | 10 | 20 | 30 | 40 | 50 | 60 | 70 | 80 | 90 |100 |
           ↑                                           ↑
           l                                           u
```

The algorithm goes as follows:

Guess where the number is by selecting the middle element. The midpoint can be determined by `midpt = ( l + u) // 2`. If we perform an integer division it doesn't matter whether we start with an even number or odd number of elements. In this case our initial mid-point will be element 5. We now have 3 possibilities:

1. `number == num[midpt]`   // Element is found.

2. `number < num[midpt]`   // Search left sub-list

3. `number > num[midpt]`   // Search right sub-list

If the number has been found, the function should return the position of this element. This is given by the value of midpt.

To search a left sub-list, we need to reposition u, so that it now points to the index with a value of midpt − 1.

To search a right sub-list, we need to reposition l so that it points to the index with value of midpt + 1.

The following illustration shows what happens if the number is found to be less than the one obtained at the mid-point.

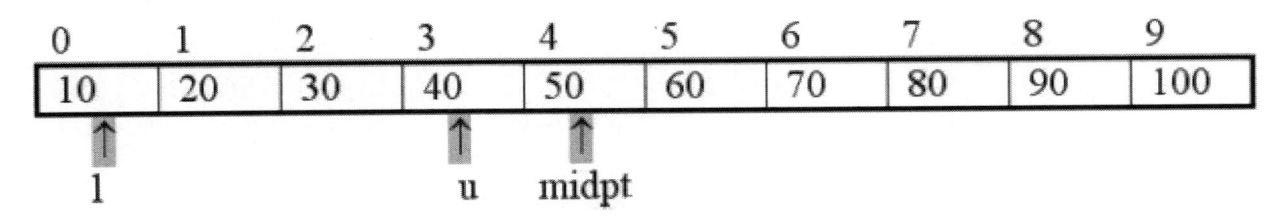

```
   0    1    2    3    4    5    6    7    8    9
 | 10 | 20 | 30 | 40 | 50 | 60 | 70 | 80 | 90 |100 |
   ↑                   ↑    ↑
   l                   u   midpt
```

The new mid point can now be calculated with the expression `[l + u] // 2` which gives us the value 2 in the diagram above. A comparison of `num[midpt]` is made to see whether the element is found etc. This is repeated until either the desired data item is found or u > l.

A completed function is given below.

```
def bsearch(a, x) :
    l = 0
    u = len(a) - 1
    while l < u :
        midpoint = (l + u) // 2
        if x == a[midpoint] :
            return midpoint
        elif x < a[midpoint] :
            u = midpoint - 1
        else :
            l = midpoint + 1
    return -1                          # Indicate failure

#   Test the function
numbers = [10, 20, 30, 40, 50, 60, 70, 80, 90, 100]
num = 110
result = bsearch(numbers, num)
if result != -1 :
    print(num, " was found at index position ", result)
else :
    print(num, " not found")
```

14.3 Bubble sort

Sorting is much more complicated than searching and involves many more comparisons. For this reason we will look at the simplest of sorts and leave a more detailed analysis until later. The simplest sort is the **bubble sort**. It contains two components, comparison and interchange. Adjacent elements of an array are compared to see if they are in the correct relative position. If not, they must be swapped round.

A strategy for doing that is as follows:

```
If a[j] > a[j+1]:
    int temp = a[j]
    a[j] = a[j-1]
    a[j-1] = temp
```

You will notice that a temporary variable called temp is used. This is necessary because the contents of a[j] are overwritten by the contents of a[j+1]. So, before you carry out this assignment, you need to save the value of a[j] somewhere.

Now a systematic means of ensuring that all elements are compared is required. A bubble sort compares adjacent elements for the entire array, swapping elements that are out of place 1 at a time. This is achieved by using a pair of nested for loops.

Before I write the program I want to work out what will happen on paper. For this purpose I will use a very small list of numbers as my sample data.

Consider the list a = [4, 5, 3, 1, 2]

For the first pass of the data, I have the following.

```
     j  j+1              j  j+1              j  j+1              j  j+1
     ↓   ↓               ↓   ↓               ↓   ↓               ↓   ↓
[4,  5,  3,  1,  2]  [4,  5,  3,  1,  2]  [4,  3,  5,  1,  2]  [4,  3,  1,  5,  2]
    No change            swap items           swap items           swap items
```

At the end of the first pass, we have [4, 3, 1, 2, 5]. You will notice that the largest number in this list is now in the correct position.

In the second pass, we repeat what we have previously done. And, at the end of the second pass, the second largest number will be in its correct position.

The actions I have just described are to be carried out within an inner for loop. To repeat these actions for multiple passes, we need an outer loop. A completed program with a function called bSort() is shown below. I have tested it using the sample data used above. I have also left in a print statement to display the state of the list after each pass. It is currently commented out, but if I wanted to use it, all I have to do is remove the comment.

```
def bSort(a) :
    for i in range(len(a)) :
        for j in range(len(a) - 1) :
            if a[j] > a[j+1] :
                #   Swap items
                temp = a[j]
                a[j] = a[j+1]
                a[j+1] = temp
        print(i, a) #   This has been left in to show results of each pass
    return a

a = [267, 492, 4, 600, 169, 290, 204, 752, 931, 34]
b = [4, 5, 3, 1, 2]
print("Original list")
print(b)
print("Intermediate results for each pass")
sorted = bSort(b)
print("Sorted data follows")
print(sorted)
```

The function has a nested pair of for loops. The outer for loop, is there to repeat the actions for each pass. So, with this data, there should be 5 passes. The inner loop is responsible for carrying out the comparison of adjacent numbers. If a number is found to be out of place, then the numbers are swapped.

The output for the program with the additional print statement left in is shown below. I have done this so that you can check the list after each pass of the inner for loop.

Normally, you would comment out this statement once you are confident that the function works correctly.

```
Original list
[4, 5, 3, 1, 2]
Intermediate results for each pass
0 [4, 3, 1, 2, 5]
1 [3, 1, 2, 4, 5]
2 [1, 2, 3, 4, 5]
3 [1, 2, 3, 4, 5]
4 [1, 2, 3, 4, 5]
Sorted data follows
[1, 2, 3, 4, 5]
>>>
```

Looking at the above, you will notice that the data was sorted after the 3rd pass. Despite this fact, this algorithm has to perform a fixed number of passes, and therefore takes longer than it should. It is well known that the bubble sort is very inefficient, perhaps the most inefficient of all sorting algorithms. There are things that I could have done to improve the efficiency. I concentrated on simplicity of algorithm.

14.4   Merging two lists

This section is a preparation for developing a merge sort program. We will first consider the merging of two lists. For this to be possible, it is essential that the two lists to be merged must be sorted.

Consider the lists a = [2, 3, 6, 8] and b = [1, 4, 5, 7]. We want to create a third list that combines these two lists so that each item in the list is in order. That is, create a third list c = [1, 2, 3, 4, 5, 6, 7, 8].

Merging two lists involves a comparison. Initially, the first items from lists a and b are compared. The smallest of these is added to list c.

Initially, we have this.

```
     i                  j
     ↓                  ↓
a = [2, 3, 6, 8]   b = [1, 4, 5, 7]   c = []
```

It is clear that 1 < 2, so 1 is appended to c, and the index j moves to the next element of list b. We now have:

```
     i                       j
     ↓                       ↓
a = [2, 3, 6, 8]   b = [1, 4, 5, 7]   c = [1]
```

For the next comparison, 2 < 4 so 2 is appended to the end of list c, and index i moves to the next item in list a. This continues until we reach the end of one of the lists.

When this happens, we need to add the remaining elements of the list that has not been fully accessed to the end of list c.

A completed program follows:

```
def merge(a, b) :
    i = 0               # index for a
    j = 0               # index for b
    c = []

    while i < len(a) and j < len(b) :
        if a[i] < b[j] :
            c.append(a[i])
            i += 1
        else :
            c.append(b[j])
            j += 1
    if i == len(a) :
        c = c + b[j:]
    else :
        c = c + a[i:]
    return c


a = [2, 3, 6, 8]
b = [1, 4, 5, 7]
c = merge(a, b)
print(c)
```

You can see from this program, that most of the processing is likely to take place within the while loop. The while loop terminates, when one of the indexes of the lists, points past the end of the list. Within the while loop is an `if` statement. This compares elements from one list with elements in another list. It is this `if` statement which determines which item gets copied to list c.

When the while loop has exited, it is necessary to determine which list had been fully accessed. The statement `i == len(a)` indicates that the index i for list a is now pointing past the end of the list. Consequently, in this situation, we would have to append the remaining part of list b to list c. The else part of the if statement, covers the situation that list b may have finished first.

Now, the real reason for me to cover the topic of merging lists. Many of the GCSE syllabi require you to study merge sort. An important component of the merge sort is merging lists. This will follow later.

14.5 Merge sort

Merge sort is one of the sorting algorithms that uses a divide and conquer approach to solve a problem. For any given list, the list is repeatedly divided into two halves, until they are one item lists. This is typically done recursively. See chapter 9 to read about recursive functions. The smaller lists are then merged together to form a sorted version of the original list.

To give you an idea of what is involved, I plan to demonstrate merge sort on paper using a very small list. I have also deliberately chosen the list to have length 8. So that it is easy to divide down the middle.

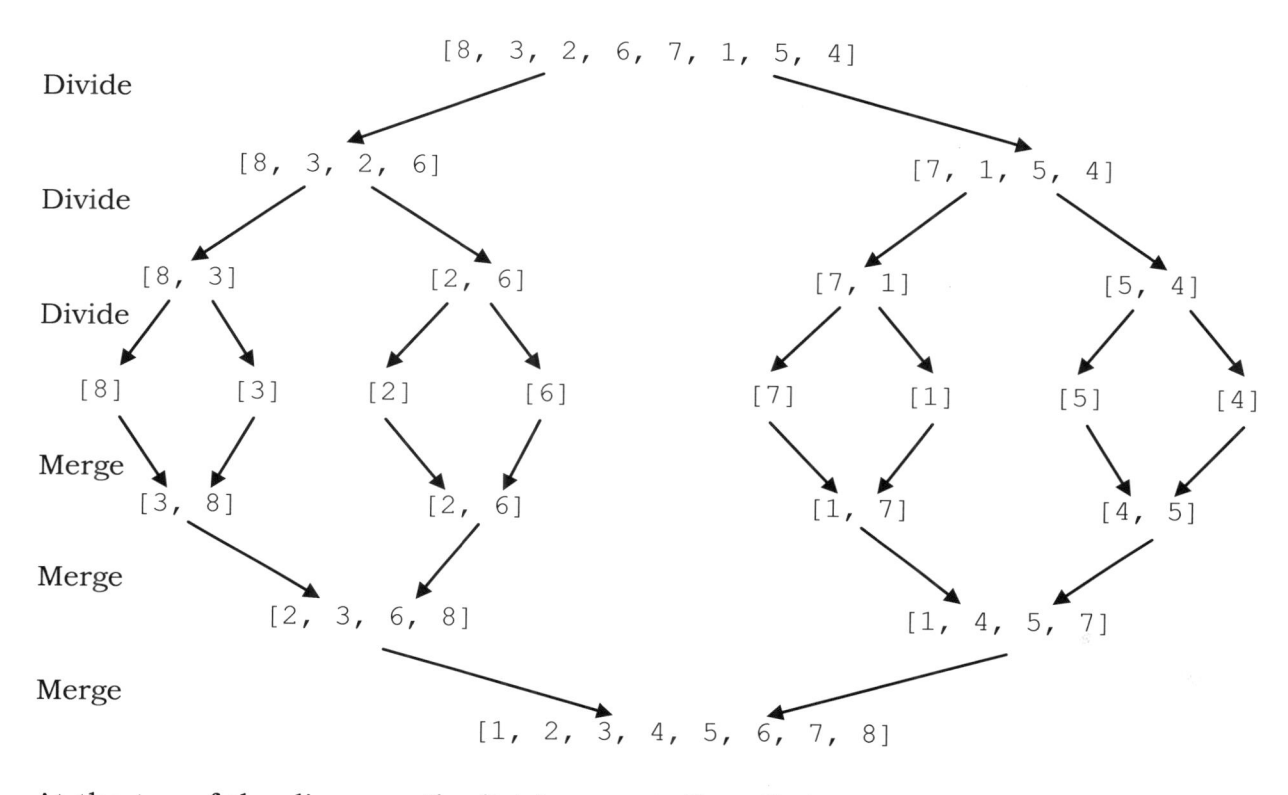

```
                        [8, 3, 2, 6, 7, 1, 5, 4]
Divide
                    ↙                              ↘
Divide       [8, 3, 2, 6]                              [7, 1, 5, 4]
             ↙           ↘                            ↙           ↘
Divide   [8, 3]         [2, 6]                    [7, 1]         [5, 4]
         ↙   ↘          ↙   ↘                    ↙   ↘          ↙   ↘
       [8]   [3]      [2]   [6]                [7]   [1]      [5]   [4]
Merge    ↘   ↙          ↘   ↙                    ↘   ↙          ↘   ↙
        [3, 8]         [2, 6]                   [1, 7]         [4, 5]
Merge        ↘         ↙                             ↘         ↙
           [2, 3, 6, 8]                           [1, 4, 5, 7]
Merge                  ↘                         ↙
                    [1, 2, 3, 4, 5, 6, 7, 8]
```

At the top of the diagram, the list is repeatedly split into two halves. At the bottom half, these small lists are merged together. Using my previous, merge() function, I can write a function called mergeSort(), that will recursively divide the list into smaller lists, and will then call the merge() function to join them back again in sorted order.

The function mergeSort() follows. You will need the merge() function for this to work.

```
def mergeSort(a) :
    if len(a) == 1 :
        return a
    else :
        midpt = len(a) // 2
        leftList = a[: midpt]
        rightList = a[midpt :]
        leftList = mergeSort(leftList)
        rightList = mergeSort(rightList)
        result = merge(leftList, rightList)
```

```
            return result

a = [8, 3, 2, 6, 7, 1, 5, 4]

sortedA = mergeSort(a)
print(sortedA)
```

The first thing I must include in the function `mergeSort()` is a terminating condition. That is, you must stop the recursive function calls, if the size of the list is 1. At this point you return the list containing a single item.

If the list is larger than 1, you continue to divide the list into left and right sub-lists. The variable midpt gives you a value for the middle. This value can then be used in conjunction with the splice operator to split the list into two halves. There are now two sub-lists, leftList and rightList. These are again used in recursive calls to divide the list again until they are reduced to single item lists.

Once the lists have been finely divided so that only single items remain, these are then merged. The final result of this merging is the value returned by the function.

I should not imagine that GCSE students would be expected to code a sorting algorithm like this. But, they are expected to know how the algorithm works. I have included it for completeness. Also, there will be some students who will benefit from this addition. Students will be expected to know how to demonstrate running a merge sort on paper with a small list as I have done.

14.6   Insertion sort

You only have to study the insertion sort if you are studying the OCR syllabus.

The insertion sort algorithm sorts a list by finding an item at a time that is out of place, and then will insert that number into its proper place. To do this, it is necessary to have a temporary variable to store this number initially. The other numbers after the number where it is to be inserted are all moved one place to the right in the list. The last of these numbers will overwrite the value that is to be moved.

To clarify this, I will have an example list that needs to be sorted.

[2, 3, 5, 7, 4, 6, 8, 1]   Here the number 4 is out of place

It needs to be inserted here. (Problem is, the 5 is in the way)

[2, 3, 5, 7, 4, 6, 8, 1]   Need to copy 4 to a temporary variable

temp ☐

Now, all the numbers to the right of 3 and to the left of 4 move 1 place to the right, starting with the number 7 which will overwrite the value 4. The value 4 which is stored in temp can now be copied to the correct position in the list.

We will now have the list:

↓

[2, 3, 4, 5, 7, 6, 8, 1]   Here the number 6 is out of place.

The procedure previously carried out before, is repeated.

We now get the following lists after each insertion has been carried out.

[2, 3, 4, 5, 6, 7, 8, 1]

And finally

[1, 2, 3, 4, 5, 6, 7, 8]

The completed insert sort program follows.

```
def insertSort(a) :
    for x in range(len(a) - 1) :
        # Find an item that is out of place
        if a[x+1] < a[x] :
            temp = a[x+1]
            pos = x + 1      # Mark position of number to overwrite
            while pos > 0 and a[pos - 1] > temp :
                a[pos] = a[pos - 1] # Move element to right
                pos -= 1
            a[pos] = temp        # Copy temp to correct position
    return a

a = [2, 3, 5, 7, 4, 6, 8, 1]

print("unsorted list is ", a)
result = insertSort(a)
print("Sorted list is ", result)
```

And, the output follows here.

```
unsorted list is  [2, 3, 5, 7, 4, 6, 8, 1]
Sorted list is  [1, 2, 3, 4, 5, 6, 7, 8]
>>>
```

14.7 Sorting algorithms profiling

AQA expects students to "Compare the efficiency of algorithms, explaining how some algorithms are more efficient than others in solving the same problem". They do not expect any formal analysis. In the main, they are interested in time efficiency.

Sorting algorithms tend to be amongst the slowest of all algorithms because they involve a huge number of comparisons. So, with large amounts of data, and even using a fast computer, a slow sort algorithm will be painfully slow. Without any analysis at all, I have carried out an experiment to test how long each of the sort algorithms will take for different size data sets.

The following code to time the 3 sorting algorithms makes use of the functions from the 3 previous sort programs. I felt there was no need to duplicate that code.

```
def createArray(size) :
    a = [0] * size
    for x in range(size) :
        a[x] = randrange(1000)
    return a

from time import time
from random import *

bubbleTimeList = []
mergeTimeList = []
insertTimeList = []

for size in [10000, 20000, 30000, 40000, 50000, 60000] :
    arr = createArray(size)
    #    Bubble sort
    startTime = time()
    a = bSort(arr)
    endTime = time()
    timeTaken = endTime - startTime
    bubbleTimeList.append(timeTaken)
    #    Merge sort
    startTime = time()
    a = mergeSort(arr)
    endTime = time()
    timeTaken = endTime - startTime
    mergeTimeList.append(timeTaken)
    #    Insert sort
    startTime = time()
    a = insertSort(arr)
    endTime = time()
    timeTaken = endTime - startTime
    insertTimeList.append(timeTaken)
```

```
print("Bubble sort times = ", bubbleTimeList)
print("Merge sort times = ", mergeTimeList)
print("Insert sort times = ", insertTimeList)
```

This program requires the use of the `time()` function from the module time. The function time returns a time in seconds. My idea is very simple. You obtain the start time before calling a sort function. After the data has been sorted, the `time()` function is called again. The difference in these values will give you the elapsed time.

I have used what I consider to be medium sized lists to store data. These data sets range in size between 10000 and 60000 items. A new dataset is created using the function `createArray()`. This function has a single parameter, the number of elements that are to be stored. The numbers stored in these lists are random numbers in the range 0 to 999.

A sample test run follows.

```
Bubble sort times =  [67.59375, 271.109375, 615.453125, 1117.953125, 1818.0625, 2667.25]
Merge sort times =   [0.15625, 0.3125, 0.46875, 0.65625, 0.828125, 1.0]
Insert sort times =  [0.0, 0.015625, 0.015625, 0.015625, 0.015625, 0.03125]
>>>
```

You can see that the bubble sort for the size of data sets chosen, is painfully slow. The times for the merge and insert sorts are very small. I was very surprised to see that the insert sort was so fast. This was totally unexpected. I knew it was faster than bubble sort, but I thought it would be much slower than merge sort. Checking on the Internet, I read somewhere that for small data sets, insert sort is even faster than quick sort. It did not say what constitutes a small data set, and I have not tested this profiling program with quick sort.

What you really want to see is a visual representation of the sort times. I have chosen bubble sort for this. I have had to use an external library that is not part of the standard Python library. The module `pylab` is contained in the library `matplotlib`. This library has to be installed separately, unless you have a python distribution such as anaconda, where this, and other libraries are installed as standard.

The following short program plots the times for bubble sort. I have rounded the times down to 1 decimal place.

```
from pylab import *
x = [10000, 20000, 30000, 40000, 50000, 60000]
y = [69.6, 271.1, 615.5, 1118.0, 1818.1, 2667.0]
xlabel("Size of List")
ylabel("Time in seconds")
plot(x, y, marker = "o")
show()
```

The output from this program follows.

```
>>>
RESTART: C:/Documents and Settings/Admin/Desktop/My Python programs/lesson14/plot2.py
```

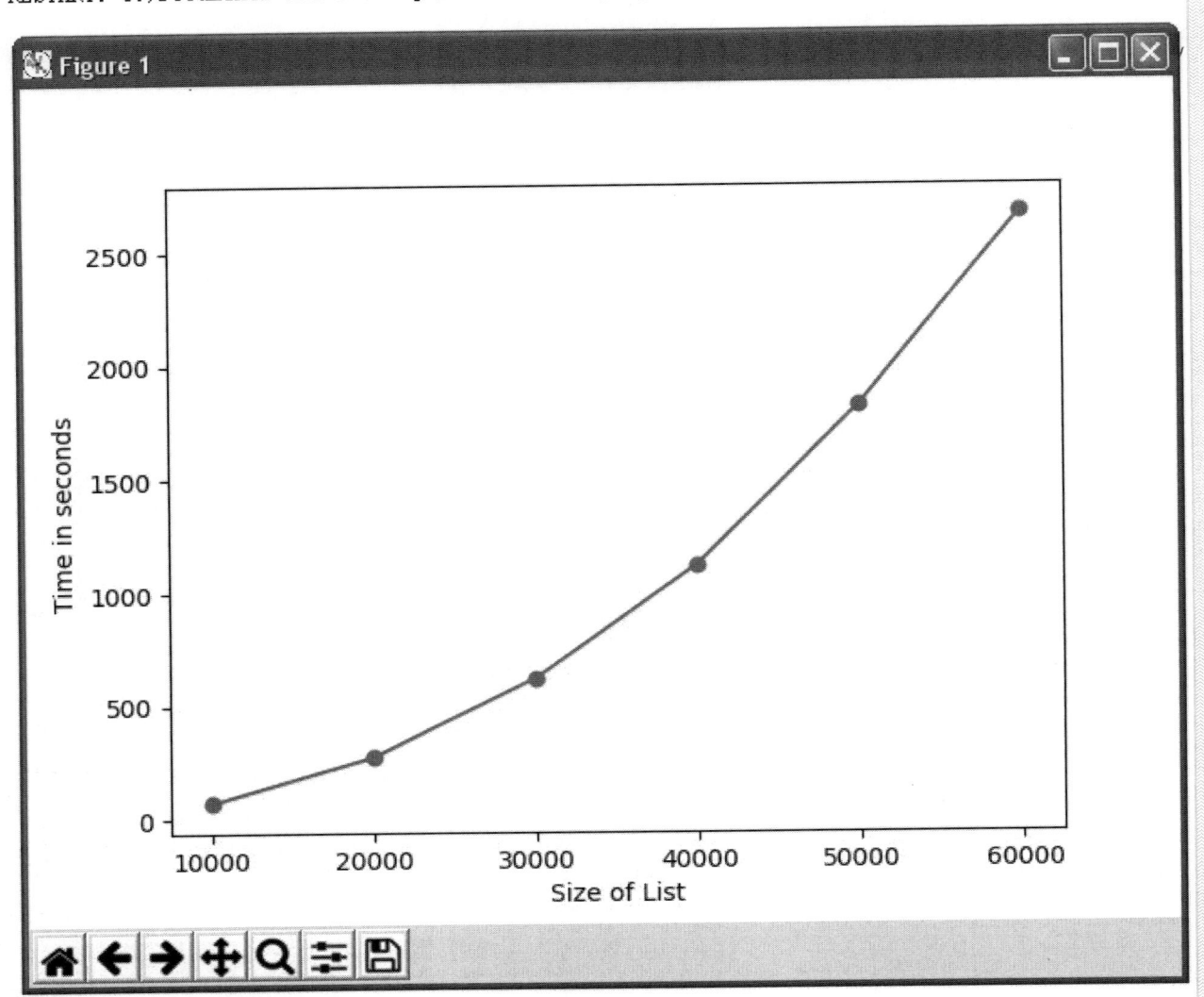

[Figure 1: Plot showing Time in seconds vs Size of List, curve rising from near 0 at 10000 to about 2700 at 60000]

The plot statement must have at least 2 parameters. Typically these are lists of numeric values. A third and optional parameter can be used to represent plotted points. The `show()` function must be called to see the plot.

You may guess that the curve plotted is a quadratic. It is well know that the complexity of bubble sort is $O(n^2)$. Informally this means that the time taken is roughly $a \times n^2$. Here a is a certain constant.

Exercise 14

1. Demonstrate on paper how the data set [3, 7, 2, 9, 1, 6, 11, 5, 4, 3] can be sorted using the different sort methods you need to study.

2. Comment on the sort algorithms. Which are the simplest to carry out. And, which are the most efficient with respect to time.

Lesson 15: Dealing with errors

15.1 Introduction

This chapter discusses debugging, testing, validation and verification, and basic error-handling.

Debugging is the process of removing faults (bugs) from a program. For debugging to take place a fault needs to be known about. Unless the fault is due to Syntax errors it is not always evident what caused the problem and where in the program that fault lies. There are however, a number of traditional techniques to help you find such errors.

Testing is the process of checking a program for correctness. It has to be systematic to increase the likelihood of finding all faults. Any moderately complex program cannot be tested exhaustively to prove the program is correct. You can however test it well enough to rid the program of most of the more blatant errors. Should the testing show up one or more errors, the program then has to be corrected.

Validation and **Verification** are techniques which are used to reject invalid data. These techniques make the program more robust so that instead of the program crashing if invalid data is entered, appropriate action can be taken (such as re-entering the data). This has already been discussed to some extent in chapter 6.

Error Handling is a catch-all phrase which covers anything else that can go wrong with the program. Despite the best intentions and efforts to produce a correct working program, there will always be the occasion when a certain set of circumstances make the program fail. Generally speaking if you have an error in your program, your program will crash with an error message. This topic deals with trapping these errors and taking appropriate action. Some of these errors may be due to hardware and so difficult to deal with until the error has been detected.

Some of the errors are easy to detect as they are due to incorrect **syntax**. Such errors are called **syntax errors**. In this case the location of where the error occurs is highlighted and it is accompanied by an error message that describes the error.

Some other errors can only be detected when the program is being run. This time it is not a question of syntax but having executed a forbidden action. These are called **run-time errors**. An example of this is dividing by zero, or an out of bounds error caused by reading past the end of an array.

The most difficult to locate are **logic errors**. These errors don't necessarily produce error messages. They do however produce the wrong results.

15.2 Syntax errors

A syntax error is a mistake in grammar. This usually involves a misspelling or expressing a statement in an incorrect format. The following illustrates one of the most common errors.

```
>>> Print("Hello")
Traceback (most recent call last):
  File "<pyshell#1>", line 1, in <module>
    Print("Hello")
NameError: name 'Print' is not defined
>>>
```

This is due to using the wrong case for a keyword. The interpreter does not know what 'Print' is, and states that it is not defined. Obviously 'print' should have been entered instead. All keywords need to be spelt correctly and in the correct case. Keywords are always in lowercase.

Missing quotes around a string is also a common mistake.

```
>>> print("Hello)

SyntaxError: EOL while scanning string literal
```

Had you type this in using the editor provided by the IDE in script mode, you possibly would not have made this mistake, because what you type in is colour coded. Having made this mistake, the error message is rather cryptic, but correct. When you declare a string, there must always be matching quotes. Here, the interpreter is scanning the entire line of code looking for another quote to end the string. It reaches the end-of-line (EOL) without finding the quote.

All statements that require a program block to be indented, must end with a colon.

```
for x in range(10)
    print(x)
```

SyntaxError: invalid syntax

As you can see, this occurred from within the IDE when I tried to run the code. It clearly indicates where the error is, but not what it is. It is up to you to know the syntax of a for statement. The first line of a for statement must always end with a colon. The same is true of if statements, while statements, and when you are defining functions.

A more difficult to detect error is incorrect indentation. This is especially the case if something is indented by a single space.

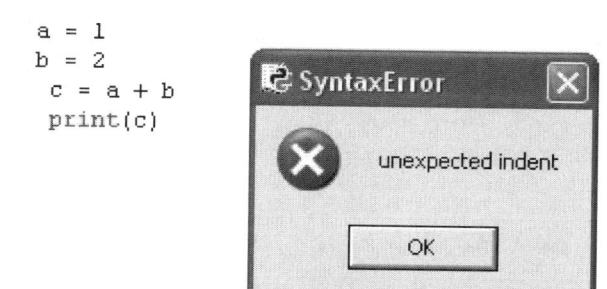

```
a = 1
b = 2
 c = a + b
 print(c)
```

SyntaxError: unexpected indent

If you get a message like this, you may need to check the indentation of all the lines of code. In this case, it is quite obvious; the last two lines of code are indented by a single character.

A very common error for many programmers, especially if they are new to programming is mistaking the assignment operator (=) for the equality operator (==). An example of this mistake follows.

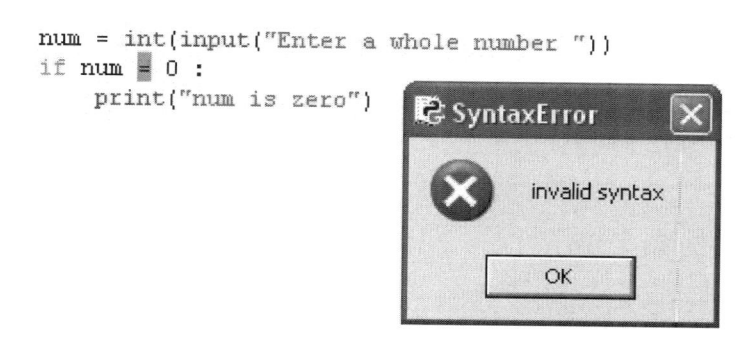

```
num = int(input("Enter a whole number "))
if num = 0 :
    print("num is zero")
```

SyntaxError: invalid syntax

Here you are told that there is invalid syntax. Also, the incorrect operator has been highlighted.

Returning to the same example with a different mistake added, we have.

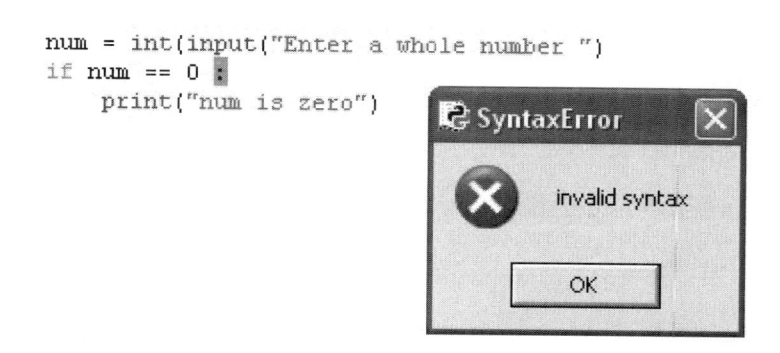

```
num = int(input("Enter a whole number ")
if num == 0 :
    print("num is zero")
```

SyntaxError: invalid syntax

Here, the error message is not clear at all. It is indicating that there is something wrong with the colon. This is not the case. Here the interpreter has got it wrong. But, you can assume that the error is nearby. Try looking at the previous statement. In this instance a right bracket is missing. A simple test to see whether the brackets match is to count left-hand brackets, and right-hand brackets, to make sure you have the same number of each.

15.3 Run-time errors

In a sense all errors in Python are run-time errors, even if they are syntax errors, because most of the time the interpreter cannot detect syntax errors until you attempt to run the program. This distinction between syntax errors and run-time errors is only ever clear when you are using compiled languages such as C or C++.

With a compiled language, you first have to **compile** the entire program. This involves checking for syntax errors before the program code can be translated into a format that can be run called **object code**. If there are errors, no object code is produced. You just get the error messages. Those errors detected in these circumstances are all syntax errors. They are also called **compile-time** errors, because this is the stage when the errors are generated.

If you do manage to compile a program, you can assume there are no syntax errors. Now, if you run a program, and it fails in some respect and generates an error message, these errors are called **run-time** errors.

So, in the context of Python, which is an interpreted language, when we talk about run-time errors, we are talking about errors that occur that become obvious whilst running a program, that are not due to incorrect syntax.

The most obvious example in arithmetic involves division by zero. The following program contains such a run-time error.

```
>>> a = 15.75
>>> b = 3.0
>>> print(a /(b - 3.0))
Traceback (most recent call last):
  File "<pyshell#4>", line 1, in <module>
    print(a /(b - 3.0))
ZeroDivisionError: float division by zero
>>>
```

This error message clearly states that we have an error because we have divided by zero. Dividing by zero is a forbidden action, because in mathematical terms, the resulting number is undefined.

Another common instance of a run-time error occurs because a user has entered incorrect data. The following has no syntax errors.

```
number = int(input("Enter a whole number "))
print(number)
```

It is dependent on the user doing as they are told, and enter a whole number. If they do not, you may result in a run-time error as illustrated below.

```
Enter a whole number 5.5
Traceback (most recent call last):
  File "C:/Documents and Settings/Admin/Desktop/My Python programs/lesson15/wron
gInput.py", line 2, in <module>
    number = int(input("Enter a whole number "))
ValueError: invalid literal for int() with base 10: '5.5'
>>>
```

The error message is quite clear. It identifies the statement that caused the problem, and identifies the error as a ValidError because invalid data has been entered. The `int()` function is unable to convert the string '5.5' to an integer.

15.4   Logic errors

These are possibly the most difficult to correct, because you do not get an error message indicating that there is something wrong with your program. You get a wrong result, which you may or may not be able to detect.

A trivial example is the following:

```
x1 = 2
x2 = 3
x3 = 4
average = x1 + x2 + x3 / 3
print(average)
```

The intended answer should have been 3.0, instead we get the following.

```
6.333333333333333
>>>
```

Here, brackets are needed to group together the numbers being summed. Instead, only the value of x3 is divided by 3. Most logic errors are not nearly so simple to detect as this contrived example.

If you run the following program it appears to do nothing.

```
price = 0.0
total = 0.0
price = float(input())
while price > 0.0 :
    total += price

print("Total is ", total)
```

There are two reasons for this. Firstly, the input statement shown provides no prompt for the user. They need to be told to enter a price and to enter 0 if they want to terminate the input. Secondly, should a user type something, it still will appear to wait because there is no second input statement. Here you have an infinite loop. The while statement will never terminate unless price is given a value of 0.

15.5 Using a trace table and other tools to test programs

A trace table is a very simple means to test your program. It is very good for detecting logic errors, and will even appear in the written exam papers. Put simply, a trace table is a table that records the value of variables at each stage of program execution.

The programmer will run the program with a set of test data and see what happens. Next, a table will be constructed on paper to record what they would expect to see if the program is run. This is also called a dry run.

By examining the program, a line at a time, the programmer records when a variable is updated. Any other variable not being updated will remain the same. When the dry run has been completed for the given set of test data, the results of the trace table are compared with the final result.

I have amended the previous program, so that the errors I have mentioned have been removed. We now have a fully working program that prompts the user for input.

I have opened the modified program in notepad++, as this editor also includes line numbers. The line numbers indicated on this program listing can also be entered into the trace table.

```
1   price = 0.0
2   total = 0.0
3   price = float(input("Enter next price (terminate with 0) : "))
4   while price > 0.0 :
5       total += price
6       price = float(input("Enter next price (terminate with 0) : "))
7
8   print("Total is ", total)
9
10
```

In this case, you will find no discrepancy between the results generated by the program and the output recorded in the trace table.

Suppose that the user enters the data:

12.75, 14.96, 5.50, 0.75, 23.25, 0

Construct a trace table to show the state of variables at each stage of execution. The trace table follows:

Line	price	total	Price > 0.0	output
1	0.0			
2	0.0	0.0		
3	12.75	0.0		
4	12.75	0.0	True	
5	12.75	12.75		
6	14.96	12.75		
4	14.96	12.75	True	
5	14.96	27.71		
6	5.50	27.71		
4	5.50	27.71	True	
5	5.50	33.21		
6	0.75	33.21		
4	0.75	33.21	True	
5	0.75	33.96		
6	23.25	33.96		
4	23.25	33.96	True	
5	23.25	57.21		
6	0	57.21		
4	0	57.21	True	
8	0	57.21		Total is 57.21

An alternative to using a trace table is the idea of adding additional print statements in the program to record the values of variables at each stage. The modified program follows:

```
price = 0.0
print("price = ", price)
total = 0.0
print("total = ", total)
price = float(input("Enter next price (terminate with 0) : "))
while price > 0.0 :
    total += price
    print("total = ", total)
    price = float(input("Enter next price (terminate with 0) : "))
    print("price = ", price)

print("Total is ", total)
```

Usually it is only necessary to add extra print statements within the loop or where you think the error may have occurred. In this case I have tried to reproduce all of the values that are updated in the trace table.

On the next page is the output generated by running this program.

```
price  =  0.0
total  =  0.0
Enter next price (terminate with 0) : 12.75
total  =  12.75
Enter next price (terminate with 0) : 14.96
price  =  14.96
total  =  27.71
Enter next price (terminate with 0) : 5.50
price  =  5.5
total  =  33.21
Enter next price (terminate with 0) : 0.75
price  =  0.75
total  =  33.96
Enter next price (terminate with 0) : 23.25
price  =  23.25
total  =  57.21
Enter next price (terminate with 0) : 0
price  =  0.0
Total is  57.21
>>>
```

This trick is often employed by programmers to help them understand why their program does not produce the desired results.

Programmers are also more likely to use tools provided by their programming environment. The most common of these is called a debugger. Python has a debugger that can be activated from the interactive shell. You activate it by clicking on Debug, then Debugger as indicated.

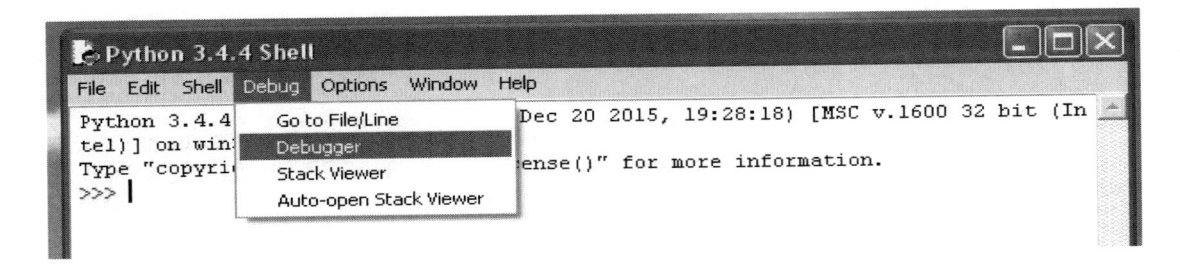

When you have done this you get a debug window.

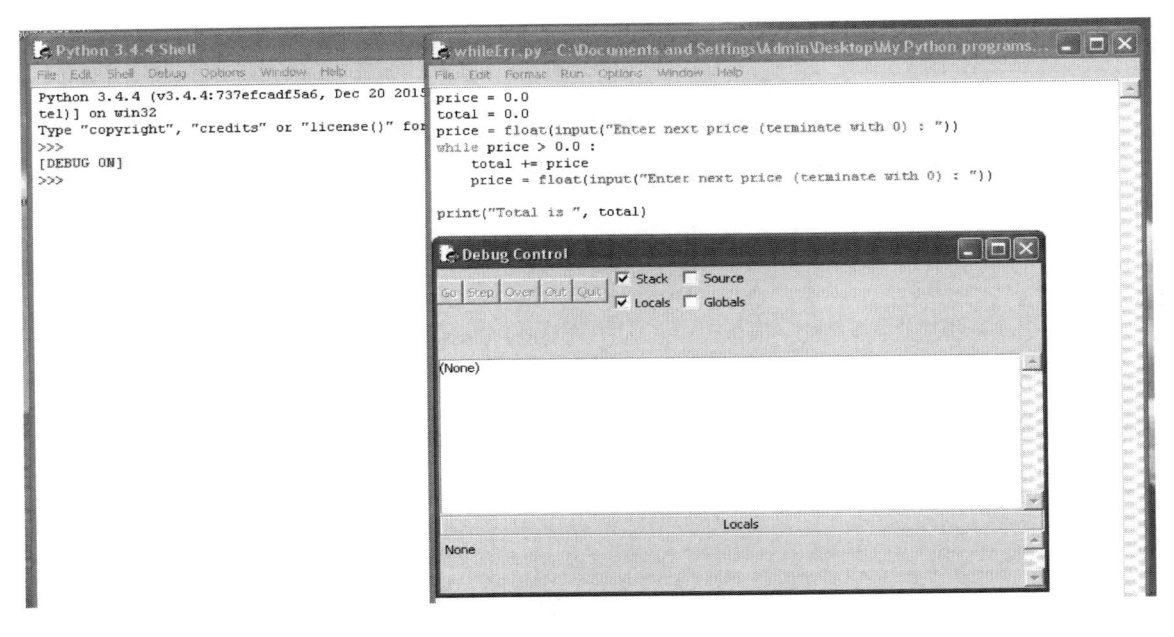

Note that I have also opened the program script that I want to debug. The next thing to do is to set a break point. You do this by selecting a line of code, and then right click on the mouse. You then obtain the following:

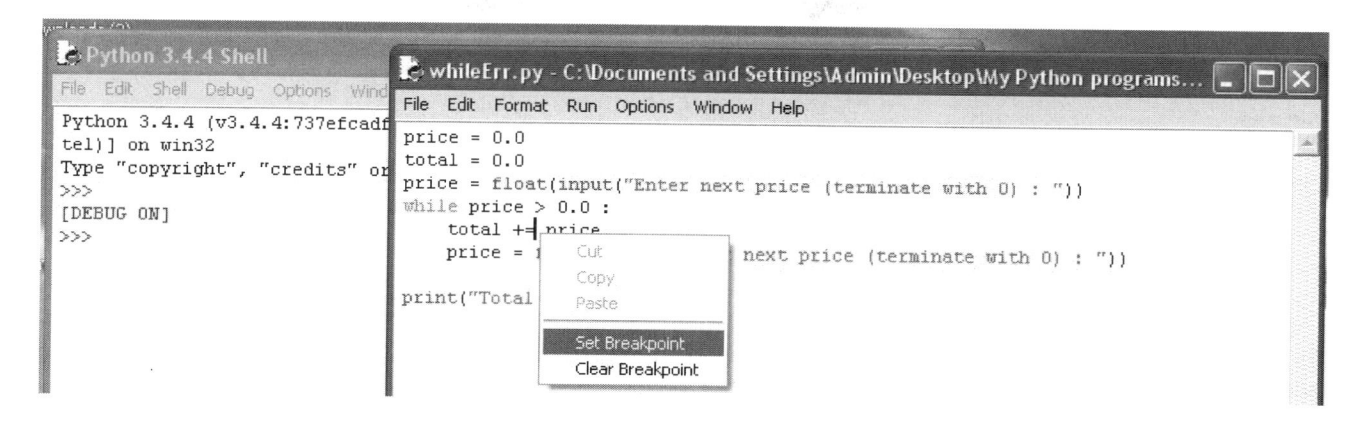

If you click on set Breakpoint, the line of code will be highlighted in yellow. Now click on run. The program will run until it reaches the line with the breakpoint. It will then displace the values of variables for this line. Initially it will give you the value of price. To continue with the debugging, click on the Step button within the Debug Control window. It will now display the value the variables one step at a time.

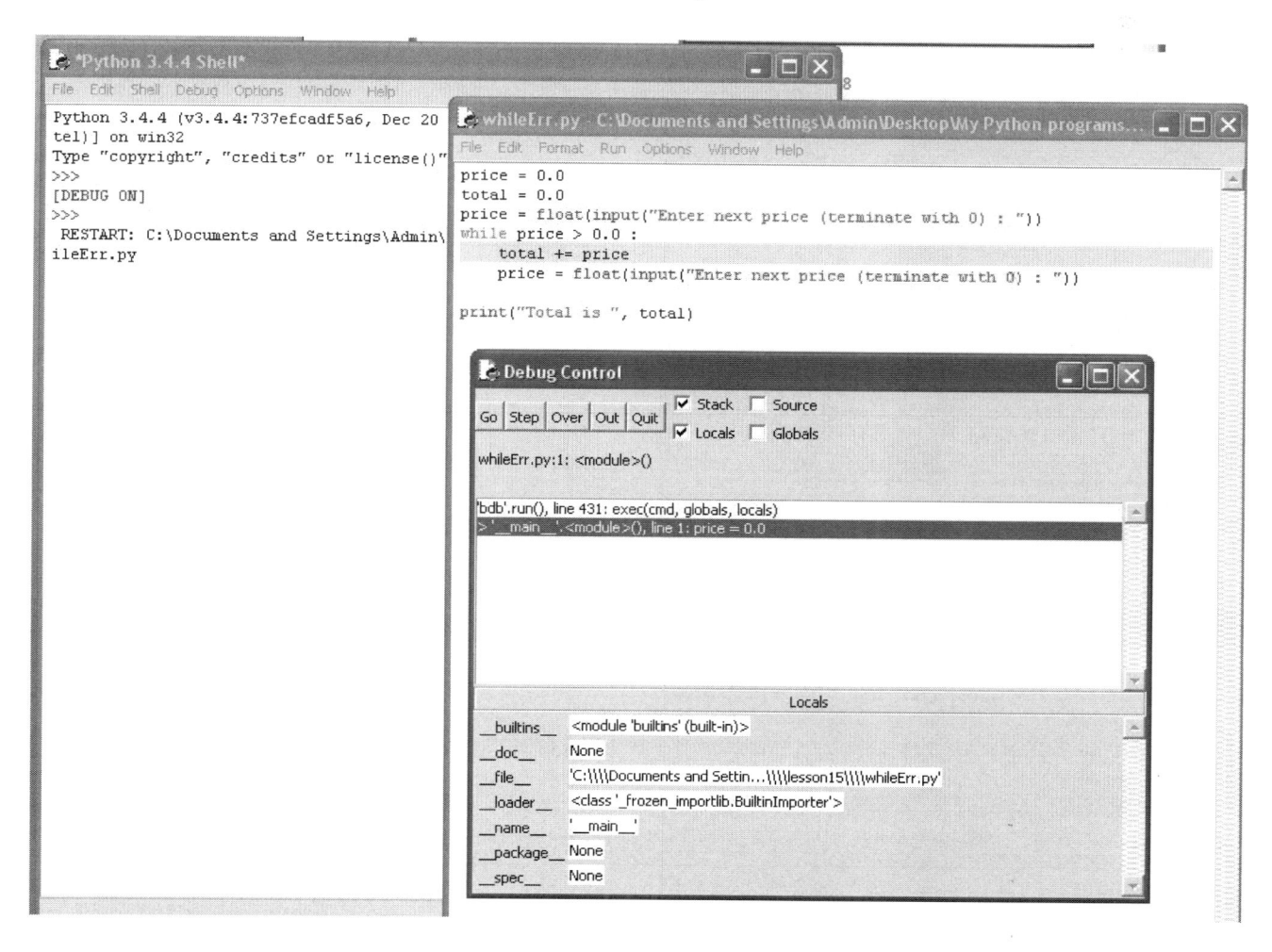

In effect, this is doing the same thing that we achieved by adding the extra print statements, but with additional information provided.

15.6 Designing a Test Plan

The aim of testing should be to intentionally create error conditions using both valid and invalid data. Invalid data should also be used to see if the program can handle them properly by validating the data etc.

For each function in the program a series of tests and test data for these tests should be determined in advance (often before the coding takes place)

The sorts of things you should consider when trying to make the functions fail are:

1. Input a number when the program is looking for a string.

2. Divide by zero.

3. Input a value outside the acceptable range.

All of these examples should be checked for within the functions. When you test the functions individually this is called unit testing.

Reasonable input should be accomplished using validation and verification. Situations like divide-by-zero can in most cases be avoided by testing the value of the divisor before division takes place. Should the divisor equal zero, then instead of letting the program crash with a system error message, you should consider printing your own error message and other diagnostics before stopping the program gracefully.

You documentation for your test plan should consists of a list of each and every test that you intend to carry out. This could be collected in a table such as the one below.

Test	Purpose	Test Data	Expected Results	Actual Results
1				
2				
3				
4				
.				
.				
.				

For unit testing you will need a table like this for each function to be tested. Likewise when you want to test the overall performance of the program you will need to create a table to document tests which will test the running of several modules at once (Integration testing).

Unit testing is the process of testing each function in isolation. This should take place as each function is being coded. After each function has been coded, you write some lines of code to test it.

The following is a simple example of unit testing. A function `numVowels()` is to be tested. This function is supposed to return the number of vowels in a given word. Besides this function, there is a test driver. You can see that this is made up of test data and function calls that use this test data.

```
def numVowels(w) :
    count = 0
    for x in w:
        x = x.lower()
        if x == 'a' or x == 'e' or x == 'i' or x == 'u' :
            count += 1
    return count


#   Test driver

#   Test data
a = "Encyclopedia"
b = "antidisestablishmentarianism"
c = "Rhythm"
d = ""

#   Tests
print("Vowel count for ", a, " = ", numVowels(a))
print("Vowel count for ", b, " = ", numVowels(b))
print("Vowel count for ", c, " = ", numVowels(c))
print("Vowel count for ", d, " = ", numVowels(d))
```

The output from this program is :

```
Vowel count for  Encyclopedia  =  4
Vowel count for  antidisestablishmentarianism  =  11
Vowel count for  Rhythm  =  0
Vowel count for    =  0
>>>
```

The results generated by the program can be verified by counting the number of vowels in each word. If there is a need for more extensive testing, a table that includes test data, as previously described should be created.

Exercise 15

Using the following flowchart create a trace table to determine the output. Use the following data sets (a) 12, 36 (b) 27, 90 (c) 250, 900 (d) 120, 1500.

Note A MOD B returns the remainder when A is divided by B.

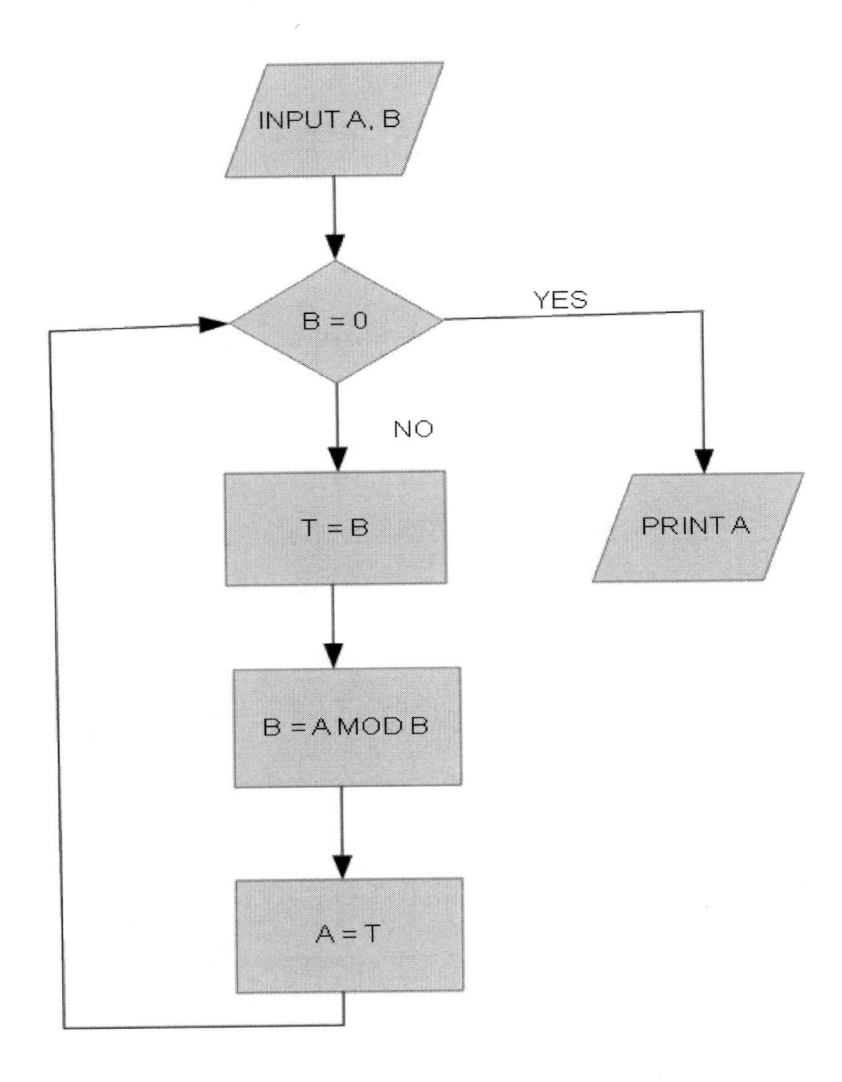

```
INPUT A, B
    ↓
   B = 0 ──YES──→ PRINT A
    │
    NO
    ↓
   T = B
    ↓
  B = A MOD B
    ↓
   A = T
    ↑ (loop back to B = 0)
```

This algorithm can be replaced by the following Python function that takes 2 parameters (a and b).

```python
def hcf(a, b) :
    while b != 0 :
        t = b
        b = a % b
        a = t
    return a
```

Show that this Python function is equivalent to the algorithm given by the flowchart. Include a test driver that uses the same data sets above and show that you get the same output as obtained by your trace tables.

Lesson 16: Non examination assessment.

This chapter contains 3 longer examples – the types of problem you may be asked to do in a non examination assessment (NEA). These examples do not include all of the features required to obtain a maximum mark.

16.1 Check for valid ISBNs

Most books have an ISBN that have 10 digits and uses a modulo 11 check digit for validation purposes. The following are examples of valid ISBNs:

1-85805-080-4
0 521 29101 1

The last digit is called the check digit and can have a value between 0 and 10. If the last digit has a value of 10, then it is represented by X.

You can determine whether you have a valid ISBN, by following these rules.

1. Each of the digits is given a weight. Starting at the right the weight is 1, to the left of this the digit has a weight of 2 and so on up to 10
2. Each of the digits is multiplied by its weight, and all of these products are summed.
3. This sum is divided by 11, and the remainder kept.
4. If all 10 digits are summed, the remainder = 0.

If an ISBN is valid, it needs to have 10 digits (once spaces and hyphens have been removed) and the sum of the digits times the weights must have a remainder of 0 when you divide by 11.

To illustrate what needs to be done, I have illustrated the calculation below.

Index	0	1	2	3	4	5	6	7	8	9
	1	8	5	8	0	5	0	8	0	4
Weight	10	9	8	7	6	5	4	3	2	1

Calculation

$Sum = 10 \times 1 + 9 \times 8 + 8 \times 5 + 7 \times 8 + 6 \times 0 + 5 \times 5 + 4 \times 0 + 3 \times 8 + 2 \times 0 + 1 \times 4$

$\rightarrow Sum = 10 + 72 + 40 + 56 + 0 + 25 + 0 + 24 + 0 + 4 = 231$

231 / 11 = 21 remainder 0

Observations

If you compare the values of the string index, and the weights, you will see that there is a simple relationship between the two. That is `weight = len(isbn) - index`.

The program needs to carry out the following, to determine whether the ISBN entered is valid.

1. Remove all hyphens and spaces
2. Check that the length of the ISBN is 10
3. Check that the characters are valid digits
4. Compute the weighted sum and find remainder modulo 11.

A suggested program follows:

```
# Remove hyphens and spaces
def removeHandS(isbn) :
    word = ""
    for ch in isbn :
        if ch != " " and ch != "-" :
            word = word + ch
    return word

# Check whether all characters are valid digits
def allDigits(isbn) :
    if len(isbn) == 10 :
        for i in range(len(isbn) - 1) :
            if not isbn[i].isdigit() :
                return False
        if isbn[9].isdigit() or isbn[9] == "X" :
            return True
        else :
            return False
    else:
        return False

# Compute weighted sum
def weightedSum(isbn) :
    sum = 0
    for i in range(len(isbn)- 1) :
        digit = int(isbn[i])
        weight = len(isbn) - i
        sum += weight * digit
    sum %= 11
    return sum

# Determine whether isbn is valid
def isValidIsbn(isbn) :
    isbn = removeHandS(isbn)
```

```
        if allDigits(isbn) and weightedSum(isbn) == 0 :
            return True
        else :
            return False

#       Test part of program
isbn = "1-85805-080-4"
if isValidIsbn(isbn) :
    print("Isbn is valid")
```

The bulk of this program is made up of 4 functions that have a specific purpose.

The function `removeHandS()` removes hyphens and spaces. The function starts with an empty string called word. Then each of the characters within isbn is tested. If they are not spaces or hyphens, the character is added to the string called word. The string word is returned by the function.

The function `allDigits()`, serves two purposes. Firstly, it checks whether the isbn has 10 digits, if not it returns False. If the ISBN does have 10 digits, there are further tests to determine whether all the digits are valid digits for an ISBN. If at any stage of the for loop, a character is found that is not a valid digit, False is returned. For the string to be a valid ISBN, all characters must be a valid digit. There is a further complication, the last character is allowed to be 'X'. This represents the number 10.

The function `weightedSum()` computes the weighted sum of all of the digits. To do this, it multiplies each digit by its weight and adds this to the total sum. The final sum is then divided by 11 to obtain a remainder. If this remainder is zero, then the ISBN is valid.

The function `isValidIsbn()` takes the ISBN as a parameter and calls the other 3 functions to determine whether the ISBN is valid. To sum up, the function calls `removeHandS()` to remove all spaces and hyphens. It then tests whether `allDigits(isbn)` is true, and also `weightedSum(isbn)` == 0. If all of these things are true, the ISBN is valid.

16.2 Binary numbers converted to base 10

The initial problem here is to design and code a program that will convert an 8 bit binary number to a base 10 or decimal number.

A binary number is a number which is composed only of binary digits or bits. A binary digit is either a 0 or 1. To think about how to carry out this conversion I must first talk about place value. The place value of a certain digit in a number is dependent on the position of that digit in the number.

We are all used to numbers being written in base 10 or decimal. For a number such as 4375, we can say that the first digit is worth 4000, the second 300, the third 70 and the last digit 5. In each case the digit has been multiplied by its place value. Starting from the right-hand-side we have units or ones. Note: $10^0 = 1$. Then as we move to the left-hand-side the place value is 10 times as large as the one on the immediate right. I have illustrated this below.

Place value 10^3 10^2 10^1 10^0

Decimal number   4   3   7   5

When considering binary numbers, the place values are all powers of 2. An 8 bit binary number is shown below with its associated place values.

Place value 2^7 2^6 2^5 2^4 2^3 2^2 2^1 2^0

Binary number   1 0 1 1 0 1 0 1

If these were to be worked out on paper, it would be normal to work out the powers of 2. So, the number we have above can be represented as follows:

Place value   128 64 32 16 8 4 2 1

Binary number   1   0   1   1   0 1 0 1

To convert the binary number to decimal, we just need to multiply the place value by the digit value and sum the results. That is:

decimal number = $128 \times 1 + 64 \times 0 + 32 \times 1 + 16 \times 1 + 8 \times 0 + 4 \times 1 + 2 \times 0 + 1 \times 1$

These ideas are to be used in the program that follows.

An initial design follows:

1.   Enter Binary number in string format

2.   Validate binary number string

3.   IF validBinary THEN
            Convert binary string to decimal integer
     END IF

To implement this initial design, I intend to use 3 functions. Done this way, you can write each function individually and then test them. The functions are:

1. `enterBinaryNumber()`

   This function just gives the user an appropriate prompt, and inputs a string into a variable called num. It is this value that is returned.

2. `validBinary()`

   This function takes as a parameter the 8 bit binary number previously input in the form of a string. It then tests that the string has 8 characters and that all of the characters are valid binary digits. If this is the case, True is returned, False otherwise.

3. `binToDec()`

   This function takes as a parameter the 8 bit binary number previously input in the form of a string. It then converts each character in the string to an integer value. These integer values are multiplied by their place value and summed. The return value is this sum.

The completed program follows:

```python
#   Enter a binary number in string format
def enterBinaryNumber() :
    num = input("Enter an 8 bit binary number : ")
    return num

#   Returns true if num is a valid 8 bit binary number string
def validBinary(num) :
    if len(num) != 8 :
        return False
    else :
        #   Test each character
        for x in num :
            if x not in ['0', '1'] :
                return False
    # Only return True if all characters binary digits
    return True

#   Returns a decimal integer given an 8 bit binary number
def binToDec(num) :
    sum = 0
    power = 7
    for x in num :
        x = int(x)
        placeValue = 2 ** power
        sum += x * placeValue
        power -= 1
    return sum
```

```
#     Test driver
n = enterBinaryNumber()
if validBinary(n) :
    decimalNumber = binToDec(n)
    print("decimal value for ", n , " is ", decimalNumber)
```

In the function `validBinary()` I have initially tested the string length of the parameter. If it is not 8, there is no point doing any further testing, so False is returned. If we have the correct string length each character must be a 0 or a 1. If anywhere in the string we find that this is not the case, False should be returned.

The expression `x not in ['0', '1']` is much easier than any other expression we could choose to see whether the digits are not one of these. It is also much easier to get the logic correct.

The algorithm for the function `binToDec()` follows the method used in the discussion at the beginning of the section. As we read a string a character at a time, each character is converted to an integer value. The digits on the left-hand-side are those that have the highest place value. For the first digit, the power is 7. So, the place value for this digit is given by *place value* = 2^{power}. Initially power has a value of 7, and this is decreased by 1 each time we loop. We start with a sum of zero. For each repetition of the loop, the place value times the digit value is added to the sum. The final sum should hold the decimal equivalent of the binary number. It is this value that is returned.

In a GCSE coursework, you probably would be expected to include an algorithm for each of the functions in this program – pseudo-code is preferable to a flowchart. I personally did not feel that this was necessary, so I left them out.

You would also be expected to put together a comprehensive test plan to test your program using a number of circumstances. The fact that the binary number string was validated in the first place means that there will be fewer chances for errors to occur.

You may want to improve what I have done. For instance, the validation function is not very user friendly. If you input an invalid string, there are no messages to tell you what you have done wrong.

16.3 Hexadecimal numbers converted to base 10

A logical extension of programming in the previous section, would be to consider hexadecimal and octal representation of numbers. I will be having a look at hexadecimal numbers, precisely because there is an added complication – there are the additional numeric digits A to F. This is because hexadecimal is base 16. Besides the digits 0 to 9, you also need A to F to be able to have 16 different digits.

In this exercise, I will be looking at 4 digit hexadecimal numbers. One hexadecimal digit can have a value of 0 to F. To represent a hexadecimal digit, 4 bits are required. So, if our program is to convert 4 hexadecimal digits, we are talking about 16 bit numbers.

I will start by looking at a 4 bit hexadecimal number in the same way that I did when investigating binary.

Let's consider the legitimate hexadecimal number 27FE.

Place value 16^3 16^2 16^1 16^0

Hexadecimal number   2   7   F   E

Given that: $16^0 = 1$, $16^1 = 16$, $16^2 = 256$, $16^3 = 4096$, we can easily work out the decimal equivalent on paper as follows:

Decimal number = $4096 \times 2 + 256 \times 7 + 16 \times 15 + 1 \times 14$

I will not be including a design for this program. It is very similar in many ways to the previous program.

The program listing follows:

```
def validHex(num) :
    if len(num) != 4 :
        return False
    else :
        #   Test each character
        hexChar = "0 1 2 3 4 5 6 7 8 9 A B C D E F a b c d e f"
        hexChar = hexChar.split()
        for x in num :
            if x not in hexChar :
                return False
    #   If I reach this far, string must be valid
    return True

#   Returns a decimal integer given an 8 bit binary number
def hexToDec(num) :
    sum = 0
    power = 3
    for x in num :
```

```python
        #   Change hex digits A to F to decimal eqivalent
        if x == "A" or x == "a" :
            x = "10"
        elif x == "B" or x == "b" :
            x = "11"
        elif x == "C" or x == "c" :
            x = "12"
        elif x == "D" or x == "d" :
            x = "13"
        elif x == "E" or x == "e" :
            x == "14"
        elif x == "F" or x == "f" :
            x = "15"
        #   Turn character to an integer
        x = int(x)
        placeValue = 16 ** power
        sum += x * placeValue
        power -= 1
    return sum


#   Test driver
n = enterHexNumber()
if validHex(n) :
    hexNumber = hexToDec(n)
    print("decimal value for ", n , " is ", hexNumber)
```

This program has 3 functions.

The function `enterHexNumber()` does not need explaining.

The function `validHex()` initially checks that the hexadecimal string is of length 4 and checks that there are only valid hexadecimal digits in the string. A character string called `hexChar` is used to store all possible valid hexadecimal characters. There is a space between each character. This is then converted to a list of possible hexadecimal characters using the `split()` method. I have used this technique to make sure that I can get everything onto one line – I do not like split lines. It is now easy to check whether or not a given character is valid. Because all of the characters need to be valid, it is important to check for invalid characters. And return False straight away. You only should return True if you have scanned the entire string and all of the characters are valid.

The function `hexToDec()` takes a hexadecimal string as a parameter and returns a decimal integer equivalent to the hexadecimal string. It sets two variables initially – sum and power. A for loop is used to pass through the string a character at a time. Within the for loop, you initially have to change all characters in the range "A" to "F" or "a" to "f" into a string that can be converted to an integer. So, "A" is converted to "10" etc. Then the character is converted to an integer using the `int()` function. Now the product of the power times the digit value is added to the sum. The final value for sum is the return value.

Like the previous program, this too is not very user friendly.

16.4 A simple film database

File processing is a very popular topic amongst exam boards. Typically they want you to be able to create a simple file that can be accessed in a number of ways. An important feature that they like to see in course work is a menu that gives the user a number of options that can be carried out.

The scenario for this programming project is that someone wants to set up a film library based on the DVDs that they have. To manage this and to keep a record of what they have, they want to have a computer system that will be able to list films according to certain criteria, and also be able to add new films to this system when they are purchased.

Initially I did some research for this. I made use of the DVDs I had at home. I also looked at some online resources such as IMDB at http://www.imdb.com/ and also INTO FILM at https://www.filmclub.org/.

My first attempt at creating a file of films was achieved using Excel. This gives an easy means to enter data and to be able to see what you are doing. A screen shot of this is shown below:

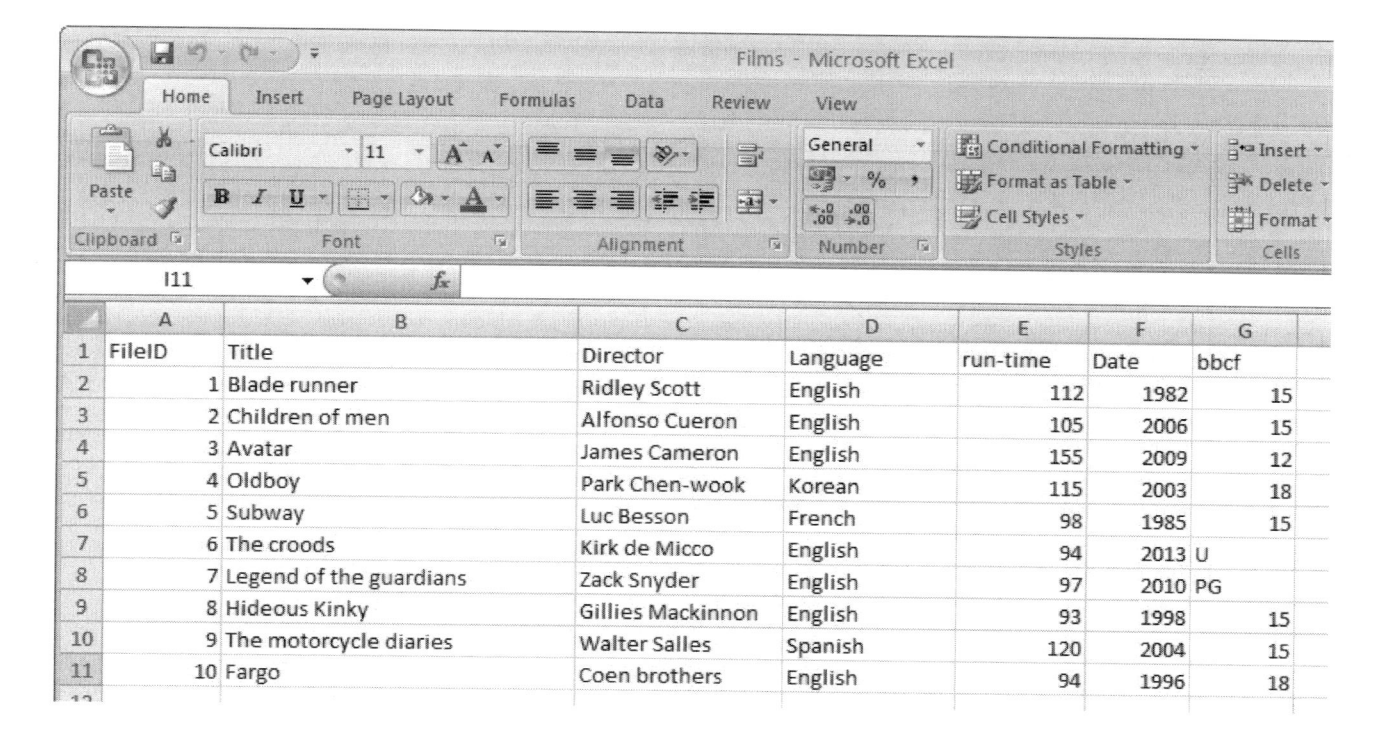

FileID	Title	Director	Language	run-time	Date	bbcf
1	Blade runner	Ridley Scott	English	112	1982	15
2	Children of men	Alfonso Cueron	English	105	2006	15
3	Avatar	James Cameron	English	155	2009	12
4	Oldboy	Park Chen-wook	Korean	115	2003	18
5	Subway	Luc Besson	French	98	1985	15
6	The croods	Kirk de Micco	English	94	2013	U
7	Legend of the guardians	Zack Snyder	English	97	2010	PG
8	Hideous Kinky	Gillies Mackinnon	English	93	1998	15
9	The motorcycle diaries	Walter Salles	Spanish	120	2004	15
10	Fargo	Coen brothers	English	94	1996	18

One of the problems that becomes apparent, is the fact that there are spaces between words in the title. The same is true of the name of a director.

We won't be able to use exactly the same methods as previously used in the chapter on files. We need a different separator between fields in a record. We could use a comma instead.

The contents of this file can be stored in CSV format. CSV stands for comma separated variable. CSV format is a very common file type shared by most spreadsheets. It is also used by many other types of software.

To save the spreadsheet above in CSV format you need to:

1. Click on Save As
2. Click on Other Formats
3. From the Save as type: pop-down menu, click on CSV(MS-DOS).

If you check the contents of your icon, you will now have another icon.

One of these contains the film data stored in CSV format. But, if you double-click on this new icon, it will be loaded up into excel and you will see exactly the same as what you did before. EXCEL obviously can read files in CSV format as well.

What you need to do is to open the file using notepad or notepad++. This way you can examine the format that the file is stored in.

To open this file using notepad you must right-click on the icon. Then choose the option Open With, then click on notepad. This is what you will see.

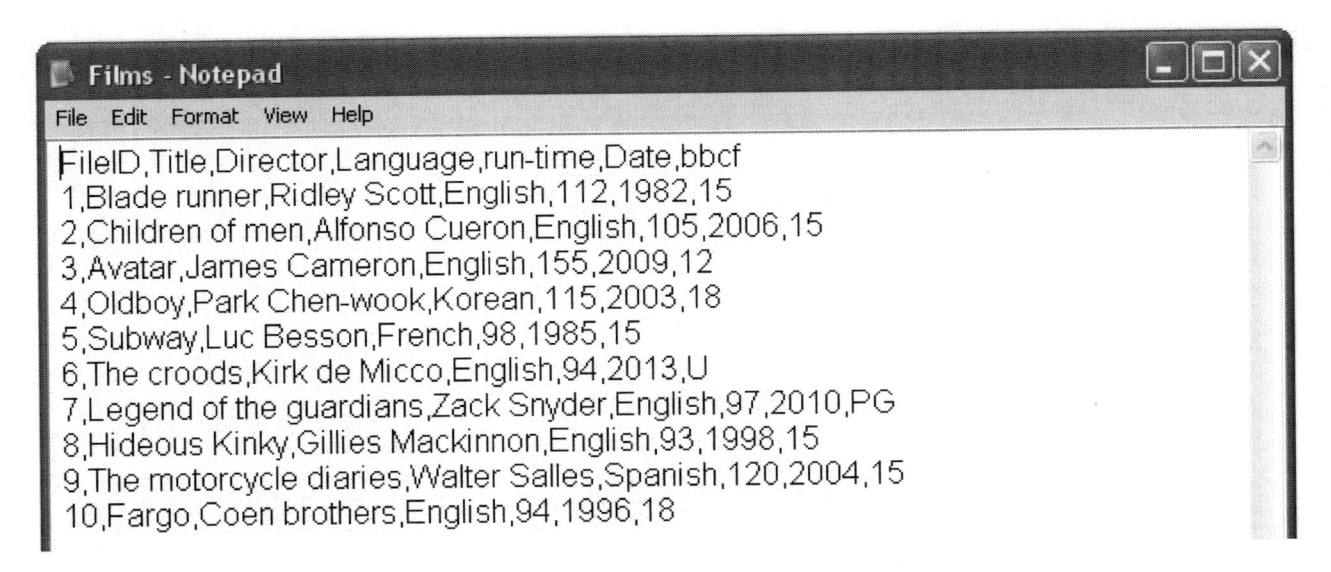

```
FileID,Title,Director,Language,run-time,Date,bbcf
1,Blade runner,Ridley Scott,English,112,1982,15
2,Children of men,Alfonso Cueron,English,105,2006,15
3,Avatar,James Cameron,English,155,2009,12
4,Oldboy,Park Chen-wook,Korean,115,2003,18
5,Subway,Luc Besson,French,98,1985,15
6,The croods,Kirk de Micco,English,94,2013,U
7,Legend of the guardians,Zack Snyder,English,97,2010,PG
8,Hideous Kinky,Gillies Mackinnon,English,93,1998,15
9,The motorcycle diaries,Walter Salles,Spanish,120,2004,15
10,Fargo,Coen brothers,English,94,1996,18
```

This file can now be saved as a text file whilst in notepad. This is a very suitable file to use for the file processing program.

Now that we have a data file. We need to consider how we are going to access the data in this file.

At this stage, I am going to do some short experiments to read and manipulate the file. The first program I wrote was:

```
infile = open("Films.txt")
films = infile.read()
print(films)
```

When I run this, I get the following output:

```
FileID,Title,Director,Language,run-time,Date,bbcf
1,Blade runner,Ridley Scott,English,112,1982,15
2,Children of men,Alfonso Cueron,English,105,2006,15
3,Avatar,James Cameron,English,155,2009,12
4,Oldboy,Park Chen-wook,Korean,115,2003,18
5,Subway,Luc Besson,French,98,1985,15
6,The croods,Kirk de Micco,English,94,2013,U
7,Legend of the guardians,Zack Snyder,English,97,2010,PG
8,Hideous Kinky,Gillies Mackinnon,English,93,1998,15
9,The motorcycle diaries,Walter Salles,Spanish,120,2004,15
10,Fargo,Coen brothers,English,94,1996,18
>>>
```

We now need to be able to access the films individually. One way to do this, that we have used previously, is to read a line at a time corresponding to a record in this file. This record can then be converted to a list using the `split()` method.

```
films = open("Films.txt")
filmList = []
for film in films :
    film = film.strip()
    film = film.split(",")
    filmList.append(film)

print(filmList)
```

In the program above, we start by creating an empty list called filmList. Then for each record in the file, we use the `strip()` method to remove the return character that is at the end of this record. Next, we use the split() method to turn this string into a list. This time we need to specify the parameter ",". This indicates to `split()` that we are to use a comma as a separator, not a space.

The list created in this way is appended to the end of the list filmList. When the for loop has completed, we will have a list that contains other lists which are the films in the file. Once this list of films has been created, this can be searched to see what films are available according to various criteria. This is a very practical way of doing things, because it is unlikely that there will be too many items to process in memory. Even INTO Film, only have around 3500 films. This is easily managed in memory.

If I run this second program, you obtain the following.

```
[['FileID', 'Title', 'Director', 'Language', 'run-time', 'Date', 'bbcf'], ['1',
'Blade runner', 'Ridley Scott', 'English', '112', '1982', '15'], ['2', 'Children
 of men', 'Alfonso Cueron', 'English', '105', '2006', '15'], ['3', 'Avatar', 'Ja
mes Cameron', 'English', '155', '2009', '12'], ['4', 'Oldboy', 'Park Chen-wook',
 'Korean', '115', '2003', '18'], ['5', 'Subway', 'Luc Besson', 'French', '98', '
1985', '15'], ['6', 'The croods', 'Kirk de Micco', 'English', '94', '2013', 'U']
, ['7', 'Legend of the guardians', 'Zack Snyder', 'English', '97', '2010', 'PG']
, ['8', 'Hideous Kinky', 'Gillies Mackinnon', 'English', '93', '1998', '15'], ['
9', 'The motorcycle diaries', 'Walter Salles', 'Spanish', '120', '2004', '15'],
['10', 'Fargo', 'Coen brothers', 'English', '94', '1996', '18']]
>>>
```

Here the output is a mess, but we can clearly see that we now have a list that contains 11 lists. The first list contains a header record that tells us what is in each of the fields. Then, this is followed by 10 further lists that contain information about 10 films.

It is now time to come up with a basic design that allows us to search the films. This and the programming will be much easier if you go for a modular programming approach. That is, just about everything will be done using functions.

The approach I have taken is to initially read the entire file. For each record read the contents is split into a list. This list is then appended to a list, which will when I have finished, contain all of the films in the file in list format. That is I have a list of lists.

It is this list of lists called filmList that will be used for searching for films using certain search criteria. Having the films in main memory like this makes it easier to search for films. I do not need to read the file each time that I want to access the films because I have a copy in memory which is in a form that makes it easier to access. I only need to make further contact with the file if I am going to add new films.

Adding a new film involves the user being prompted so that they can enter the details for each field. They do not need to enter the fileID, as the fileID is just one more than the last film entered. This value can be determined from the length of the list. Once these values are obtained, two operations are performed. Firstly a list containing these values is appended to the end of the list of films called films. This means that you don't need to read the file again to do a search because all relevant information is available in memory. Secondly, These values are put into an appropriate format and then written to the file in append mode. For this to happen, the values of all of the variables need to be concatenated to form a string, making sure that a comma is placed between each item. Finally a new-line character is added to the end of the string.

The basic control structure used here is a while loop. This loop terminates when the user types Q or q to terminate. Within the while loop, the function `menu()` is called. This function displays the choices available and prompts the user to enter their choice from the menu presented.

To search for a film by title, I have assumed that the user does not know the full name. Also, I do not want to have problems with case. For that reason, both the item entered by the user, and the title in the file is converted to lowercase. I scan the films using a for loop that inspects all the records except for the first which contains the header information. Here I use the test `if filmTitle in f :` , where f is the lowercase version of the field given by `film[1]`. Use of the in operator checks whether filmTitle is a subset of the string f. In other words the film title entered by the user is part of the film title.

The same reasoning applies to searching for a film by director name. But, in the case of film classification, this is not necessary. The user is told what to enter.

The `printFilm()` function is used to print a record from the file that has been stored in the list films. If you print the very first record, you display the film header information. You will note that I have had to use a formatted print statement, as the data stored in the file is not of a fixed length. Consequently, if I want to have a neat tabular format I need to specify a field length for each data item. Within the first part of the print statement there are some format strings within curly brackets. The expression `{:30}` specifies that the item being printed should have a field length of 30.

The full program follows:

```
#       Program to manage film database

def menu() :
    print( " " * 20 + "Menu")
    print("1.      List films by British film classification")
    print("2.      List films by title")
    print("3.      List films by director")
    print("4.      List films by language")
    print("5.      Add a new film")
    print("Type Q to quit menu")
    print()
    option = input("Enter your choice or Q to quit : ")
    return option

def printFilm(film) :
    print("{:6} {:30} {:20} {:10} {:8} {:5} {:4}" \
          .format(film[0], film[1], film[2], film[3], film[4], \
          film[5], film[6]))

def readFileToList() :
    films = open("Films.txt")
    filmList = []
    for film in films :
        film = film.strip()
        film = film.split(",")
        filmList.append(film)
    films.close()
    return filmList
```

```python
def displayByFilmClass() :
    filmClass = input("Enter British Film Classification : ")
    printFilm(films[0])
    for film in films :
        if film[6] == filmClass :
            printFilm(film)

def displayByTitle() :
    filmTitle = input("Film title : ")
    filmTitle = filmTitle.lower()
    printFilm(films[0])
    for film in films :
        f = film[1].lower()
        if filmTitle in f :
            printFilm(film)

def displayByDirector() :
    filmDirector = input("Film Director : ")
    filmDirector = filmDirector.lower()
    printFilm(films[0])
    for film in films :
        f = film[2].lower()
        if filmDirector in f :
            printFilm(film)

def displayByLanguage() :
    filmLanguage = input("Film Language : ")
    filmLanguage = filmLanguage.lower()
    printFilm(films[0])
    for film in films :
        f = film[3].lower()
        if filmLanguage == f :
            printFilm(film)

 def addNewFilm() :
    filmID = len(films)
    filmID = str(filmID)
    title = input("Enter title of film : ")
    director = input("Enter director of film : ")
    language = input("Enter language : ")
    runTime = input("Enter film run-time (mins) : ")
    dateMade = input("Enter date produced : ")
    bbfc = input("Enter film classification (U, PG, 12, 15, 18) : ")
    film = [filmID, title, director, language, runTime, dateMade, bbfc]
    films.append(film)
    outFilms = open("Films.txt", "a")
    outString = filmID + "," + title + "," + director + "," + \
                language + "," + runTime + "," + dateMade + \
                "," + bbfc + "\n"
    outFilms.write(outString)
```

```
        outFilms.close()

#   Read file into a list of films called films
films = readFileToList()

option = "Start"
while option != "Q" and option != "q" :
    option = menu()
    if option == "1" :
        displayByFimClass()
    elif option == "2" :
        displayByTitle()
    elif option == "3" :
        displayByDirector()
    elif option == "4" :
        displayByLanguage()
    elif option == "5" :
        addNewFilm()
```

Below I have output to show searching for a film by director.

```
                    Menu
1.    List films by British film classification
2.    List films by title
3.    List films by director
4.    List films by language
5.    Add a new film
Type Q to quit menu

Enter your choice or Q to quit : 3
Film Director : Besson
FileID Title                    Director        Language   run-time Date  bbcf
5      Subway                   Luc Besson      French     98       1985  15
```

Below I have include output to show what happens if you add a new film.

```
                    Menu
1.    List films by British film classification
2.    List films by title
3.    List films by director
4.    List films by language
5.    Add a new film
Type Q to quit menu

Enter your choice or Q to quit : 5
Enter title of film : A clockwork orange
Enter director of film : Stanley Kubrick
Enter language : English
Enter film run-time (mins) : 136
Enter date produced : 1971
Enter film classification (U, PG, 12, 15, 18) : 18
```

Exercise 16

Rather than write new programs, I would like you to modify the programs that I have written. In particular, it would be a good idea to extend the programs and make them more user-friendly.

1. The function `isValidIsbn()` in section 16.1 is a pure function that does one of two things. It returns true if the ISBN is valid and false otherwise. If the ISBN entered is invalid, there are no messages to tell us that. One way of dealing with this problem is to add side-effects to the function. That is, if it returns false, you should introduce print statements to indicate why the ISBN is not valid.

2. In section 16.2, the function `enterBinaryNumber()` allows a user to entire 8 bit binary number in one go. A common problem with this approach is that too many or too few digits are typed. To get round this problem, you could use a loop to enter one digit at a time. If you use a for loop, this can be used to count 8 digits. Rewrite the function so that a user enters a binary digit one at a time as described.

3. Using the ideas obtained in sections 16.2 and 16.3, write a program that will convert an octal number (base 8) into decimal (base 10).

4. In section 16.4 there is a file processing program that uses a single file film.txt. Extend this program so that a DVD can be lent out. Rather than modify the existing film file, you could create another file that records the loans. This can be called loans.txt. Each time a film is loaned you need to write a record to the file loans.txt. It should have the following format: fileID, userID, date. Note, when you want to borrow a DVD, you first have to do two things. Firstly, the film must be in the film file. Secondly, you have to make sure that it has not been borrowed already.

5. This program can be extended further by creating another file that contains user details. A suggested file format is: userID, userName, telephoneNo, email. So if in question 4 you identify a loan where a user has not returned the film after a week, you can locate their details and contact them.

   You will note that the file formats used in section 16.4 and questions 4 and 5 correspond to a simple relational database. This would suggest that such a problem might be best tackled using a relational database management system.

Appendix A

Bibliography

Python programming

1. Downey, Allen B. Python for software design: How to think like a computer scientist 1/e. Cambridge University press 2009.
2. Horstmann, Cay & Necaise, Rance. Python for everyone 2/e. Wiley 2016.
3. Langtangen, Hans Petter. A Primer on Scientific Programming with Python 5/e. Springer Verlag 2016.
4. Lee, Kent D. Python programming fundamentals 1/e. Springer Verlag 2011.
5. Lutz, Mark. Learning Python 4/e. O'Reilly
6. Perkovic, Ljubomir. Introduction to computing using Python: An application development focus 1/e. Wiley 2012.
7. Sweigart, Al. Automate the boring stuff with Python: Practical programming for total beginners. No starch press 2015.

GCSE / IGCSE Python

1. Dawkins, Patrick. GCSE Python: a guide to the practical component 1/e. Lulu 2013
2. Roffey, Chris. Cambridge IGCSE and O level Computer Science programming book for Python 1/e. Cambridge University press 2017.

GCSE Computer Science

1. Cushing, Steve. AQA GCSE (9-1) Computer Science 1/e. Hodder Education 2016.
2. Cushing, Steve. Edexcel Computer Science for GCSE (9-1) 1/e. Hodder Education 2016.
3. Harman, N. GCSE Computer Science – Theory and Practice: Python powered for Edexcel 2018 1/e. Createspace 2016.
4. Waller, David. GCSE for OCR Computer Science 1/e. Cambridge University Press 2016.

GCSE Mathematics

1. Norman, Naomi & Pate, Katherine et al. Edexcel GCSE (9-1) Mathematics Higher 1/e. Pearson 2015
2. Morrison, Karen & Smith, Julia et al. Higher mathematics GCSE for Edexcel 1/e. Cambridge University press 2015.

Online books in PDF format

1. Downey, Allen. Think Python: How to think like a Computer Scientist 2/e. Green Tea press 2015. http://greenteapress.com/thinkpython2/thinkpython2.pdf
2. Sweigart, Al. Invent with Python. https://inventwithpython.com/chapters/

Appendix B

Resources

Software

Python software foundation	https://www.python.org/
Python	https://www.python.org/downloads/
Matplotlib library	https://pypi.python.org/pypi/matplotlib
Online Python tutor	http://pythontutor.com/

Installation(How to)

Install Python	https://www.howtogeek.com/197947/how-to-install-python-on-windows/
Install Matplotlib	http://matplotlib.org/users/installing.html

Exam boards

AQA GCSE Computer Science
http://www.aqa.org.uk/subjects/computer-science-and-it/gcse/computer-science-8520

EDEXCEL GCSE Computer Science
https://qualifications.pearson.com/en/qualifications/edexcel-gcses/computer-science-2016.html

OCR GCSE Computer Science
http://www.ocr.org.uk/qualifications/gcse-computer-science-j276-from-2016/

Programming practice

Learn Python tutorial	http://www.learnpython.org/
Using Python	http://usingpython.com/
Project Euler archives	https://projecteuler.net/archives

Index

A

`acos()` function 108-109
algorithm 117
algorithmic complexity 140
analysis 123-124
and 33
`append()` method 58-59, 163
arrays 85-94
array processing 87-88
arguments (See parameters)
arithmetic operators 4, 11-12
ASCII characters 26, 126
ASCII code 26, 31
`asin()` function 108
assignment 15
assignment operators 15, 68-70
assignment statement 15-17
associativity of operators 14-15
`atan()` function 108

B

binary 156
binary digit (bit) 156
bisection search 130-131
block 47, 48
Bohn & Jacopini 39
`bool` class 30
`bool()` function 36
Boole, George 30
Boolean constant 30
Boolean expressions 30-31
Boolean Type 30
break statement 70-71
breakpoint 70-71
bubble sort 131-132
byte 15

C

calculate change 43-45
calculator 4
call by value 74
calling functions 74
camel case 19
case-sensitive 19
case statement 49
casting 34
character 29
character representation 26, 31
check digit 153
`chr()` function 27

classify a vertebrate 117
`close()` method 96
comma separated variable 162
command prompt 3
comment 18
compile time errors 144
concatenate operator + 22, 58
concatenation 22
conditional statements 47-55
control variable 63, 86
converting seconds to days, hours, minutes and seconds 17
`cos()` function 107
`count()` method 60
CSV format 162
cubic equation 112-114

D

data terminator 68
data types 29
days in a month 52-54
debugger 148-149
debugging 141
declaring an array 85-86
declaration of functions 74
declaration of variables 15
`def` keyword 74
`degrees()` function 108
dichotomous key 118
dry run 143

E

editor 5
elif 48-49
else 48-49
empty list 59
empty string 58
`end = ""` to prevent a new-line 71
equality operator (==) 30-31, 33, 52-54
error handling 141
errors 141-145
EXCEL 161
Exponentiation 11

F

`fabs()` function 113
factorial 72, 82-83
False 30
Fibonacci numbers 91
files 95-104

float 4
float class 34
`float()` method 34
floating point number 4
flow charts 37-38, 117-121, 152
folder 1
for loops 63-66
forced conversion 34
formatted output 165
function body 74
function call 74
function definition 74
functions 73-84
functions that return a value 74-76
functions that have no return value 76-78
functions that process arrays 88-89
functions that process files 102-103
functions that return an array 90-91

G

global scope 79
global variables 79
goto statement 118
graphic user interface (GUI) 3

H

`help()` 9, 19
hexadecimal number 159

I

IDE 3
IDLE 3
IDLE shell 3
`if` statement 47-48
`if ... elif ... else` 48-49, 53-54
import statement 106, 139
immutable 23
in operator 23, 154, 159, 166
indentation 48
index (arrays) 85, 86
index (lists) 85, 86
index (strings) 21
index operator [] 21, 22, 57
input 39-40, 41
`input()` method
`insert()` method 59-60
insertion sort 136-137
int class 30
`int()` method 35, 36, 98-99
integer 4
integer division 12, 18, 43-45

interactive programming 3
interpreter 3
`isalnum()` method 26
`isalpha()` method 26
ISBN 153-155
`isdigit()` method 26
`islower()` method 26
`isspace()` method 26
`isupper()` method 26
iteration 63-72
iterative formula 112-113

J

Jackson structure programming (JSP) 125-128

K

Keyboard input 39
Keywords 19

L

left-to-right associative 14
`len()` 25, 27, 59
length of list 59
length of string 25, 27
linear search 129
lists 57-62, 85-94, 133
local scope 79
local variables 79
logical expressions 33
logical connectives 33
logic error 141, 145-146
loop 63-72
`lower()` method 25, 32

M

math module 14, 106
mathematical functions 106-108
`matplotlib` library 139, 170
`max()` 59
mean 88
median 89-90
merge sort 135-136
merging two lists 133-134
method 25
`min()` 59
modulus operator (%) 12, 18, 43-45
Monte Carlo simulation 111-112
multiplication table 66, 71

multiply operator (strings, lists) 24, 27-28, 61, 85, 86

N

nested if statements 51
nested loops 71
non exam assessment (NEA)
not 30
notepad 5, 162
notepad++ 145
numerical solution of cubic equation 112-114
numerical solution of a quadratic equation 70

O

octal 168
`open()` method 95, 97, 99
or 30
`ord()` function 27, 29
order of operations 13-15
ordinal number 27
output 39

P

palindromes 80-81
parameters
    actual parameters 77
    formal parameters 77
pi 106
`plot()` function 139, 140
powers 11
`pop()` method 59, 60
precedence of operators 72
prime numbers 114-115
probability 109
procedure 73
processing 39
procedural programming 37
program design 122, 124-128
program trace 146-147, 152
pseudo-code 119, 121, 125
`pylab` module 139
Pythagoras' theorem 111
Python 1
Python shell 3, 21, 31

Q

quadratic equations 41-43, 49-50

R

Radians 107
`radians()` function 108
`random()` function 111, 112
random numbers 109-112
range check 50
`range()` function 61-62, 65-66
`randrange()` function 110
`read()` method 96
`readline()` method 97
real division 4
real number 4
recurrence relation 82, 112, 116
recursion 82
recursive function 82-83
relational operator 30-31
remainder operator % 11, 18, 43-45
`remove()` method 60
return value 73
`reverse()` method 60
right-to-left associative 15
`round()` function 42
`rstrip()` method 97, 98
run-time errors 42, 141, 144-145

S

Scientific notation 105
scope 79
script mode 5-8, 18
selection 38, 47-55
sequence (sequential programming) 37
`show()` function 139, 140
sieve of Eratosthenes 114
`sin()` function 107
slice 22, 58
`sort()` method 60
sort profiling 139-139
special characters 24
specification 123
`split()` method 160, 163
`sqrt()` 14, 106
standard form 105
stepwise refinement 124
str class 25, 35, 39
`str()` method 35
strings 4, 18-28
string comparison 31-32
string functions 25
string methods 25-26
string slicing 22
structure chart 124
subscript operator [ ] 11

substrings 22
`sum()` function 59
swap items 132
syntax errors 18, 141, 142-143
system stack 83

T

`tan()` function 107, 108
temperature conversion 16, 40
terminating input using a data
    terminator 68
test plan 150-151
testing 122
testing with extra print statements
    147-148
`time()` function 138-139
times table 66, 71
top-down design 124
trace table 146-147, 152
trigonometry 107-109
True 30
truth tables 33
two dimensional arrays 92-93
type casting 34
`type()` function 29, 30

U

unit testing 151
`upper()` method 25

V

validation 50-51, 141
variable 15
variable assignment 15
variable declaration 15
variable names 19
verification 51-52, 141

W

Wittgenstein, Ludwig 33
while loop 72-73
white space 17, 30
`write()` method 99-101

Printed in Great Britain
by Amazon